YOU SAY YOU WANT
A REVOLUTION?

You Say You Want a Revolution?

RADICAL IDEALISM AND ITS TRAGIC CONSEQUENCES

DANIEL CHIROT

PRINCETON UNIVERSITY PRESS

PRINCETON & OXFORD

Published by Princeton University Press
41 William Street, Princeton, New Jersey 08540
6 Oxford Street, Woodstock, Oxfordshire OX20 1TR

press.princeton.edu

ISBN (e-book) 9780691199900

Library of Congress Cataloging-in-Publication Data

Names: Chirot, Daniel, author.
Title: You say you want a revolution? : radical idealism and its tragic consequences /
Daniel Chirot.
Description: Princeton, New Jersey : Princeton University Press, [2020] |
    Includes bibliographical references and index.
Identifiers: LCCN 2019018027 | ISBN 9780691193670 (hardcover)
Subjects: LCSH: Revolutions—History. | Revolutions—Philosophy.
Classification: LCC JC491 .C475 2020 | DDC 303.6/409—dc23
LC record available at https://lccn.loc.gov/2019018027

British Library Cataloging-in-Publication Data is available

Editorial: Peter Dougherty and Alena Chekanov
Production Editorial: Lauren Lepow
Jacket Design: Layla MacRory
Production: Erin Suydam
Publicity: Alyssa Sanford and Kate Farquhar-Thomson

This book has been composed in Arno Pro

Printed on acid-free paper. ∞

Printed in the United States of America

10 9 8 7 6 5 4 3 2 1

To my grandchildren, Eric and Chloe. I hope that by the time they are old enough to understand what this book is about, the world will be freer than it is today of the threat that such tragedies will once again occur.

CONTENTS

Acknowledgments ix

1 Revolution as Tragedy   1

2 Incompetence, Chaos, and Extremism:
How More Moderate Forces Lost Control in
France, Russia, Iran, and Germany   12

3 Reaction, War, Invasion, and Revolutionary Terror   36

4 The Tyranny of Idealistic Certitude and
Imagined Utopias   63

5 Revolutions Betrayed: Autocratic Corruption
and the End of Idealistic Third Worldism   105

6 Peaceful Revolutions? Interpreting Conservative
and Liberal Successes and Failures   118

7 Are There Lessons for Us to Learn?   127

Notes 135
Index of Cited Authors 159
Subject Index 163

ACKNOWLEDGMENTS

I NEED TO THANK a few close friends and colleagues who have helped me improve this book. They are not, of course, responsible for any remaining errors or biases that they have tried to correct and for which they cannot be blamed.

Zoltan Barany, Lucian Leustean, and Ivan Berend carefully read the manuscript and made useful suggestions that guided some of my revisions. My University of Washington colleagues Reşat Kasaba, Vanessa Freije, and Mark Metzler also helped.

It is common to thank family members, but two actually read everything and provided many challenging, insightful criticisms that helped me. My wife, Cynthia Chirot, and my daughter, Laura Chirot, devoted a lot of time to greatly improve my writing.

Two anonymous reviewers and members of the Princeton University Press Board also added suggestions that I have taken seriously and used to make some necessary additions. I am very grateful to the superb editorial staff at the Press, and particularly to Lauren Lepow's tremendously detailed, insightful copyediting.

I have relied in the past on Scott Smiley's excellent indexing skills, and want to thank him again.

Once again I must thank Herbert J. Ellison's family and the George F. Russell, Jr., family for their support in endowing a professorship in honor of my late colleague Professor Ellison. My research and writing have greatly benefited from the help provided by this professorship.

Most of all I have to thank my friend and editor Peter Dougherty. I cannot praise his dedication and hard work enough. I am not the only author he has immensely helped in his long career, so I join his other admirers in saying that those of us who have been fortunate enough to benefit from his recommendations and help owe him a great debt.

YOU SAY YOU WANT
A REVOLUTION?

1

Revolution as Tragedy

It seems as if the doctrine that all kinds of monstrous cruelties must be permitted, because without these the ideal state of affairs cannot be attained—all the justifications of broken eggs for the sake of the ultimate omelette, all the brutalities, sacrifices, brain-washing, all those revolutions . . . all this is for nothing, for the perfect universe is not merely unattainable but inconceivable, and everything done to bring it about is founded on an enormous intellectual fallacy.

—ISAIAH BERLIN[1]

Men or groups who possess unlimited power become drunk on that power . . . in no circumstances is unlimited power acceptable, and in reality, it is never necessary.

—BENJAMIN CONSTANT[2]

ON MARCH 29, 1794, the imprisoned Marie Jean Antoine Nicolas de Caritat, marquis of Condorcet, died, probably poisoned. It was a tragedy, not only because France lost one of its greatest-ever thinkers, but also because his death symbolically marked the ultimate collapse of liberalism in the French Revolution. Was it suicide to escape being guillotined, or was he murdered by the Jacobin revolutionary authorities who had ordered his arrest? He had been hiding for months but had finally been caught on March 27. His death two days later spared the government the embarrassment of publicly murdering one of the early heroes of the 1789 Revolution, known as a leading philosopher throughout Europe.

Condorcet was an outstanding, versatile Enlightenment philosopher. He was a great mathematician, a defender of women's rights who considered women to be men's intellectual equals at a time when such an opinion was rare, a strong proponent of democracy, and an adversary of slavery. His brilliant thinking about economics, politics, and history was in tune with Adam Smith's liberal ideas. He was a very well-connected nobleman close to the most reformist members of France's royal government before 1789. Recognizing the need to modernize the monarchy and make politics more inclusive, he nevertheless accepted the revolution and became one of its early leaders. Skeptical of religion, believing in the perfectibility of human societies, Condorcet was the ultimate rational liberal. Though his ideals were for his time radical, he was opposed to the bloodshed, terror, and extreme, polarizing means that the radical Jacobins used once they gained power, and that is why they condemned him to death.[3]

Condorcet's tragic end at the hands of extremists was a violent act that would be replicated over and over in the great revolutions of the twentieth century, from Mexico's in 1910 to Iran's in 1979. The reason is that the great revolutions all had something in common. Most sidelined and typically purged the first wave of more moderate revolutionaries.

Almost two years before Condorcet's death, in mid-August 1792, the Marquis de La Fayette, also one of the early leaders of the French Revolution as well as a heroic figure in America because of his youthful service in its revolution, fled France. On August 14 Georges Danton, the minister of justice in the new radical Jacobin government, had issued a warrant for his arrest. The Jacobins considered La Fayette to be a defender of the monarchy, and untrustworthy. To save himself from a certain death sentence, he crossed over into Austrian territory (in what is now Belgium, but at that time ruled by the Austrian Habsburgs). The Habsburgs were then France's main enemy and sought to save Louis XVI and his Habsburg wife, Marie-Antoinette. Because La Fayette had participated in the revolution, led some of its armies, and was considered to be a dangerous, radical antimonarchist, he was arrested and held in prison for five years. In fact, he was neither the reactionary monarchist the Jacobins saw, nor the drastically antiroyal revolutionary the monarchists and their European allies thought he was. He was, instead, the quintessential moderate liberal reformer who had tried to mediate between the demand for more democracy, in which he passionately believed, and King Louis XVI, whose life and throne he wanted to preserve. He thought that a limited, constitutional monarchy was the solution. He admired the kind of democratic limitations on executive power the Americans were pioneering with their new Constitution. But the king and his court never willingly accepted his proposals and decided La Fayette was a traitor to the monarchy. On the contrary the more radical revolutionaries distrusted moderation and felt that La Fayette was really an ally of antirevolutionary reaction and foreign intervention.[4]

There are lessons to be drawn today from what happened to Condorcet and La Fayette, particularly at times when political extremism once again rejects rational, moderate solutions to political, social, and economic problems. By looking at revolutions of both the right and the left and considering why so many slid into destructive extremism, I hope to show by the end of this book what we can gain by studying them.

The La Fayette Syndrome: Liberals Beware

La Fayette was certainly not the intellectual equal of Condorcet, and his enemies considered him a self-serving mediocrity. Nevertheless, at the start of the revolution he was one of the leading liberal aristocrats, was very popular, and was given command of the National Guard. In trying to protect the royal family while remaining true to his democratic inclinations, he was willing to use force to control extremism. So he gradually lost the trust of the revolutionary Parisian masses and of the men he commanded. His fall, which will be discussed in more detail below, was actually a turning point that foreshadowed the Reign of Terror and all that entailed, including the murder of not just Condorcet but many other luminaries—including, eventually, Georges Danton himself, who had issued the warrant for La Fayette's arrest.

La Fayette and Condorcet's dilemma, to be caught between intransigent resistance to reform by the king and royal court and equally uncompromising revolutionary radicalism, is the danger commonly faced by liberal moderates; but it is particularly acute in the kinds of chaotic environments that produce revolutions. Francisco Madero, the first president of Mexico after its revolution began in 1910, and also Russia's Alexander Kerensky, the major leader of the 1917 Russian Revolution before the Bolsheviks seized power, suffered the same fate for similar reasons. The former was murdered by an antirevolutionary general, and the latter fled into exile when Lenin's Bolsheviks overthrew him. Shapour Bakhtiar, the liberal politician who ushered the shah of Iran into exile in 1979, was subsequently repudiated by Ayatollah Ruhola Khomeini and also had to flee into exile. Iranian government agents eventually murdered him in Paris.

The quandary faced by moderates does not always end in their defeat. Great Britain industrialized, went through drastic social change, and democratized in the nineteenth to mid-twentieth century without a revolution. Nevertheless, when established institutions are failing and societies become too dramatically polarized—as happened in the revolutionary situations we are going to examine in this book—La Fayette's and Condorcet's failures look like the probable fate of those like them who tried to steer a middle course in turbulent times. That is as true today as it was in the French Revolution. Why?

The classical liberalism that emerged from Enlightenment thinking in the eighteenth century, and has remained since then at the core of democratic moderation and progress, relies on a few basic assumptions. The most important is that there are scientific truths that can be discerned in both the natural and the human world, and these should be deployed to devise policies to better society. But discovering these truths is not easy and requires constant questioning and revision as new evidence becomes available. This is difficult. Humans are not naturally predisposed to live with the uncertainty of always reexamining reality; nor do they always understand what is best for them. Economic laissez-faire claims that private interests in competition with each other will yield more efficient and generally beneficial economic outcomes. The underlying assumption about the value of democratic politics is similar. Allowing competing political goals to peacefully compete will let the best win, if not at first, then eventually as publics learn what is better or worse. That is the fundamental theory behind democracy. For Condorcet democracy would work because, according to the laws of probability, a properly enlightened public would eventually come up with a majority in favor of the best solution.[5]

What liberalism finds hard to cope with is fanaticism that relies on a fixed, unchangeable idea so certain of itself that it is closed to rational testing. In other words, liberal skepticism about any definitive solution is unable to persuade those who reject science itself. Nor can liberalism easily counter systematic lying if that is done skillfully enough to persuade people to deny evidence that runs counter to their beliefs. To any moderate, not only liberal ones but also conservatives, extremist ideology too often seems preposterously unreasonable. So the danger is recognized too late. In a well-educated, relatively stable society with freedom of expression and a basic faith in science, the fanatics and liars can be marginalized. But when these beneficial conditions no longer exist, and when at the same time critical problems can no longer be successfully handled, moderate reformism will no longer prevail.

La Fayette may not have been the great philosopher and writer that Condorcet was, but he had an innate faith in reason and the power of democratic consensus. In France after 1791 his belief that his nation could find the right political balance between the extremes of reaction and radical change resulted in the kind of blindness that might be labeled the "La Fayette syndrome." This illusion has destroyed many a moderate, more liberal proponent of democratic change in revolutionary times.

Revolutions, Progress, and Bad Outcomes

"Revolution" is so widely used a word that I should explain how I will use it in this book. Revolutions are inspired by ideals that call for the building of a better society by deliberately and quickly changing, at a minimum, key political rules and institutions. In most but not all cases the intention is also to transform economic and social relations. Revolutions have leaders who do not place much faith in gradual, piecemeal reforms. Gradual reform of legal, economic, and social institutions and habits may over time produce changes as drastic as actual revolutions, but those kinds of relatively slow evolutionary transformations will not be considered actual revolutions.

All important changes meet some opposition from people defending their interests, but when revolutionary transformations threaten to upend a whole political or social order, resistance is almost certain to provoke violence. There have been a few notable cases when violent reaction was avoided; but almost all of the examples used in the book, including the best-known modern revolutions since the late eighteenth century, turned into civil wars. While a few exceptions will be discussed toward the end of the book, such anomalies cannot negate the more common occurrence of widespread revolutionary and counterrevolutionary violence.

Generally, however, the early stages of revolutions, as in France, began less radically and at least somewhat more peacefully. But the first wave of more moderate, typically liberal reformers were ousted. The first stage was therefore not the end point but only the first in a series of developments that ultimately led to revolutionary tragedies. Of course if you believe that human history is generally a march toward greater progress despite occasional backsliding, you might not agree that the outcomes of the most dramatic revolutions were headed for catastrophe once the moderate reformers were sidelined. You believe instead that the great revolutions since the late eighteenth century were necessary if often painful steps that had to be taken when progress was blocked by reactionary political and social forces. That is how Marxist theory and practice interpret history. Most non-Marxist progressives who might decry the excessive bloodiness of Stalinism and Maoism still think that the Russian and Chinese revolutions were necessary and ultimately positive steps.

That is what liberal thought eventually settled on in interpreting the most paradigmatic of all modern revolutions, the French one of 1789. It turned into a brutal civil war that killed hundreds of thousands. It ended with Napoleon's military dictatorship that caused about a million French war deaths and several times that among other Europeans. Napoleon set France back economically and demographically so badly that it fell behind its main European rivals and never really caught up. Marxists think that the French Revolution went wrong when its most radically egalitarian Jacobin activists lost power in the Thermidorian reaction of 1794 against the Reign of Terror, and even more with Napoleon's coup d'état on the 18th of Brumaire at the end of 1799. But at least, so the claim goes, it broke the bonds of feudalism in much of Europe and so allowed capitalism to progress and thrive. Liberals who hate the memory of the Jacobin Reign of Terror in 1793 and 1794 basically agree that despite all its failings, that is exactly what the French Revolution did, and that therefore it allowed the rise of a new kind of freer, more rational, more progressive society. Undoubtedly all of the great revolutions, like the French one, occurred in societies that badly needed more reform than those in power were willing or able to grant, so of course they can be justified by their supporters. Our question, however, is whether so much violence could have been avoided to produce better long-term outcomes. Was all that suffering really necessary? Did the ends justify such drastic means?

Americans do not argue as much about the consequences of their revolution of 1775– 1783 and mostly see it as an unambiguous success. But by leaving in place its ruling social classes, the American Revolution left unsolved the problem of slavery. That eventually caused the vastly bloodier Civil War of 1861–1865. The failure after that to deal satisfactorily with the legacy of racism has ever since bedeviled the United States. So even the American Revolution's obvious success in creating what would become the modern world's first democracy also failed in some important ways. Nevertheless, understanding why it was not immediately as bloody or disruptive as the subsequent French Revolution can tell us much about why so many later revolutions turned so quickly into tragedies.

After the first modern revolutions in the late eighteenth century, the American and French, the most momentous have been in the twentieth century. The Russian, Chinese, and other successful communist revolutions were inspired by Marxism and killed tens of millions in order to achieve an impossible egalitarian ideal. Mexico's somewhat less studied revolution that began in 1910 and lasted ten years—or longer, according to some—slaughtered hundreds of thousands. The Iranian Revolution of 1979 created a uniquely theocratic regime unlike any previously known. It too has been bloody and ultimately corrupt as it has tried to spread its brand of radical Islam beyond its borders. Many if not all of the anticolonial revolutions in the second half of the twentieth century wound up creating authoritarian, repressive, corrupt regimes in much of Africa, the Middle East, and Southeast Asia.[6]

To the list of catastrophic revolutions it is necessary to add transformative fascist regimes, particularly Nazism. Hitler and Mussolini may have been helped to power by conservatives hostile to communism and to more moderate social democracy, but both dictators intended to seriously revolutionize their countries by creating original, totalitarian social orders with new fascist political elites. Hitler went about this much more thoroughly than did Mussolini, though he had less time in power and was defeated long before completing the transformation. It is too easy to simply dismiss fascist idealism as mere reactionary hostility to social change combined with extreme imperial ambitions. On the contrary the extreme, aggressive brutality of fascism was as much a part of the tragic twentieth century's revolutionary legacy as was communism.[7]

Understanding fascism's radical goals and why it can attract support is particularly relevant today because, since the demise of European communism, most of the rising radicalism in Europe and much of the rest of the world is tending toward a new kind of fascism.

It does have to be said that despite the tragic consequences of so many revolutions, it is not only inaccurate but also morally obtuse to deny that most of them, even the most violent, were justified, at least at first. If so, why did they descend into so much destructive violence?

The Four Acts of Revolutionary Tragedies

What follows will not consist of case studies divided into separate country chapters on their own. Rather, four main revolutionary stages, mirroring in some ways the dramatic progression of classic tragedy, will be treated in the four chapters that follow this one. Supporting evidence from some key revolutions will be used as appropriate to better illuminate and explain each stage. This means that sometimes important examples, most obviously those taken from the French and Russian revolutions, will be used in different chapters. For example, the Russian Revolution moved from the first, liberal reformist act to an early form of idealistic if brutal Leninism. There followed a third, even more deadly Stalinist phase, and finally a slow slide into inefficient corruption and loss of revolutionary fervor. Not all revolutions follow all four of these stages, but some do, and all experience at least two or three of them.

1. Revolutions occur when existing elites fail to solve major problems and lose confidence in themselves so that order breaks down. In the ensuing chaos political actors with little governing or administrative experience become the new governing elite. Typically they are relatively moderate but as a result fail to satisfy or even fully understand the demands and anger of many who back radical change. Their failure opens the way to a next wave of revolutionaries, who are more ruthless and do not hesitate to use more violent means to seize and hold power.

2. Counterrevolutionary reaction leads to increasingly contentious politics and often civil war, foreign intervention, or both. To stay in power, the new power holders need to enhance and reinforce their repressive institutions; otherwise they are likely to be overthrown. The military and police apparatuses built up by radical regimes are then available to further the revolutionaries' hold on power.

3. Radical revolutionary leaders tend to hold unrealistic views about how malleable people and societies really are; therefore, they insist on pushing unworkable ideals. When these do not work, if the leaders possess strong repressive tools, they will use violence to force recalcitrant populations into line. They also cast blame on outside states and organizations, internal treachery, or some combination of both. Blaming others allows the radical idealists to deny that their original programs were fundamentally flawed from the start. This leads not only to greater repression, but also very commonly to purges within elite ranks as the need to identify scapegoats increases.

4. Committed revolutionaries are loath to give up their idealistic goals, but eventually, if they keep power long enough, they or their successors begin to make compromises. Repressive,

nontransparent regimes become increasingly corrupt because they lack corrective institutions that might expose their transgressions. Corruption and the abandonment of many if not all revolutionary ideals may happen quickly or slowly over time. The upshot is the same. Corruption becomes another mark of failure and may redouble repression to conceal it.

Another way to view this summary is as a chart. Not all of these developments need exist or operate together in sequence in every case, but at least several of these categories and their effects are typical of most revolutions and account for their ultimately disastrous outcomes.

How Repressive Revolutionary Extremism Develops

Four Stages of Revolutionary Transformations	Internal Causes	External Influence
How the radicals come to power	Old regime incompetence creates chaos. Moderate liberals prominent at first don't grasp the situation and fail to quiet discontent.	Sometimes foreign powers dominate the social system directly, as in colonies, or indirectly, and help block reform.
How a repressive apparatus is built up and becomes permanently institutionalized	Counterrevolutionary civil war, threat of one, or fabrication of this danger allows radicals to increase repression.	Real foreign intervention, or exaggeration of that threat, even if fabricated, permits institutionalization of the repressive apparatus.
Radical utopianism	The ruling party's idealism leads it to refuse to admit its program's limitations, so repressive violence becomes necessary to carry it out.	Excluding outside influence and information to keep the population unaware of the real situation becomes an essential repressive tool.
Gradual slide into corruption	"Thermidorian" reactions occur soon or later.* The relaxation of revolutionary momentum opens the way to corruption, but the repressive institutions block correction.	As the population is more exposed to the outside, awareness of failure and corruption increases, but this requires more repression to keep the elite in control.

*"Thermidorian" reaction refers to the moderation of revolutionary violence and zeal after the French Revolution's Reign of Terror.

To explain how these stages occur and what effects they have, I will draw examples from particularly relevant cases.

Before we turn to detailed analysis, it is worth noting that in the original modern revolutions, the American and the French, the former avoided all of the listed outcomes, but the latter fell into every one of these traps. That is one reason that, ever since, the French Revolution's history has become a paradigm used repeatedly by analysts of more recent revolutions.

This book has two objectives. One is to explain the dynamics of revolutions. The other is to account for why they so often turn out tragically. To accomplish this goal, the next four chapters will elaborate on each of the stages in the chart. Then chapter 6 will offer some counterexamples that show how the most radical outcomes are hardly inevitable and can sometimes be avoided, though moderation itself may be unexpectedly destabilizing in the longer run. A final, seventh, chapter will suggest that we might be able to draw some conclusions from all this for contemporary use.

2

Incompetence, Chaos, and Extremism

HOW MORE MODERATE FORCES LOST CONTROL IN FRANCE, RUSSIA, IRAN, AND GERMANY

Ah! ça ira, ça ira, ça ira	Ah, it'll all be fine, fine, fine
les aristocrates à la lanterne!	The aristocrats to the lamp-post
Ah! ça ira, ça ira, ça ira	Ah, it'll all be fine, fine, fine
Les aristocrates on les pendra!	The aristocrats, we'll hang them
Et quand on les aura tous pendus	And when we've hung them all
On leur fichera la pelle au cul	We'll shove a shovel up their ass

—POPULAR FRENCH REVOLUTIONARY SONG THAT WAS THE UNOFFICIAL ANTHEM BEFORE "LA MARSEILLAISE"[1]

The Soviet regime has acted in the way that all revolutionary proletariat should act; it has made a break with bourgeois justice. . . . For as long as we fail to treat speculators the way they deserve—with a bullet in the head—we will not get anywhere at all.

—VLADIMIR ILYICH LENIN[2]

THE FIRST ACT of major revolutions typically saw more moderate forces in the ascendant. In 1789 France, 1917 Russia, and 1979 Iran these were liberal reformers. A quite different example was Germany in 1932–

1933 when most thought that a right-wing, nationalist army was about to take control with the aim of restoring something close to the pre-1918 conservative imperial regime. Instead, a much more radical, genuinely revolutionary Nazi Party took power. However distinct this was from other revolutions, it was similar in this respect: it took an unanticipated extreme form that very few had foreseen. Hitler changed Germany in ways unsought by either the left, the moderate center, or the incompetent conservatives who had lost control.

Conservative Resistance, Liberal Failure, and the Rise of France's Radical Revolutionaries

The French government's incompetence and its aristocracy's foolishness in the 1780s turned a manageable fiscal crisis into a revolution whose consequences almost no one had foreseen. Then what began in 1789 as a series of reasonable and necessary reforms degenerated into catastrophic violence. This was followed by a partial but uninspired and faltering recovery that delivered the final blow, Napoleon's warmongering military dictatorship. Before we proceed to other examples, it is worth reviewing what that revolution was and what it was not.

Despite its archaic administrative inefficiencies, France in the early 1780s was still the most powerful state in Europe. With about twenty-eight million people, it was the second most populated country in Europe after a Russia that had only recently surpassed it but was much poorer and, across its much larger area, sparsely populated. France had had contiguous boundaries for centuries, and it had far fewer ethnic, linguistic, and cultural cleavages than Austria, its main continental rival. Its total economic output was also the largest in Europe. Britain was pulling ahead of France with the start of the Industrial Revolution, and it had more efficient finances, agriculture, and political institutions. But even counting its troubled, agriculturally backward colony of Ireland, Britain's population was only about half of France's. France was still the leader, along with Great Britain, in the European-wide scientific and philosophical Enlightenment. The French state, therefore, should have been able to draw on significant economic and human resources to solve its problems. Revolution was neither anticipated nor inevitable.[3]

If France had resources adequate to meet its problems, it was, nevertheless, a deeply troubled society. Its state was practically bankrupt. Outdated institutions and calcified, hereditarily based status distinctions blocked reform. The traditional basis of royal and religious legitimacy had been badly undermined among both noble and bourgeois elites by the Enlightenment, which mocked religious superstition and called for a more democratic, more rational political system. At a more popular level repeated economic problems and bad harvests in the 1770s and 1780s generated protests because of food shortages that severely affected the 85 percent of the population that was still rural. The rising price of bread, the staple food in the towns as well, engendered widespread urban unrest because of rumors that hoarders connected to the aristocracy and royal court were responsible. The late 1780s were particularly bad because of the weather, and 1788 was the worst of it.

The costly wars of Louis XIV (reigned 1643–1715) and his feckless successor Louis XV (reigned 1715–1774), along with the successful but also expensive war against Britain under Louis XVI (reigned 1774–1792) to help the American War of Independence, had created enormous debts. To this was added the very expensive maintenance of the extravagant royal court of Versailles established by Louis XIV and continued under his successors.

The state's increasingly unmanageable finances could not be fixed without fiscal reform to raise more money from the privileged upper segments of the nobility and the ruling lords of the Catholic Church. The nobility and the church still owned or controlled about 45 percent of French lands, and they could draw on various customary revenues that were partly holdovers from retrograde feudal obligations that no longer made much sense. In fact, feudalism as such, a society based on all-powerful rural nobles ruling dependent serfs, had mostly disappeared long before, to be replaced by a very mixed combination of large estates, tenants, paid workers, small and medium peasant holdings, and bourgeois property.[4]

By 1787 the state was desperately looking for solutions, but few thought that the monarchy itself was on the edge of collapse. It certainly could have been saved.[5]

The aristocracy throughout the eighteenth century had been fighting to regain the political powers it had lost during Louis XIV's absolutist reign. Nobles used their status and assistance from the thirteen high courts called *parlements* (judicial institutions not to be confused with the English Parliament) to block reforms, hoping to thereby force the monarchy to give them more control. Paradoxically the defenders of noble interests against royal absolutism also justified their dislike of the absolutist monarchy with the Enlightenment philosophers' ideas about granting all of the people, not just elites, political liberties.[6] The aristocracy's self-confidence, but not its sense of entitlement, had been sapped by those very Enlightenment ideas. Whatever its ambitions, it lacked the institutional base that the British nobility had long been able to use to its advantage through control of the English Parliament. In 1856, analyzing the causes of the revolution, Alexis de Tocqueville tried to explain the aristocracy's astonishing political collapse in 1789: it was doomed by the lack of political responsibility and the contradiction between its wishes to retain its status and its seduction by liberal Enlightenment philosophy.[7]

The aristocracy's attempt to use the fiscal crisis to bolster its power in 1787 forced the king and his ministers to seek a solution by calling the archaic Estates-General to meet in 1788. A semiparliamentary medieval institution with no clearly defined powers or procedures, the Estates-General had not met since 1614. No one was quite sure how it should work. There were three estates, each representing one of the official orders of the realm: the nobility, the church, and the bourgeois commons. (The English version combined nobility and the church in the House of Lords, but of course the Lords and Commons were functioning, well-established parliamentary institutions far more powerful than the British monarchy, which had been definitively relegated to a more symbolic role after 1688.)[8]

After the Estates-General was called, suggestions and complaints were collected in the *cahiers de doléances* (Notebooks of grievances—

meant primarily to collect ideas for change). Delegates were then locally elected in early 1789. The entire process, however, was confused and chaotic, as there were few precedents for establishing the rules. The king agreed that the Third Estate, the commoners, could have twice as many representatives as the other orders, but the aristocracy and church would together have as many, and it seemed that each estate would have equal voting power, thus relegating the commoners to a minority of one-third.[9]

When the Estates-General met in the royal town of Versailles outside Paris on May 5, 1789, it immediately ran into trouble because the bourgeois commoners (most of whom were locally prominent provincial lawyers and other prosperous local notables) refused to accept being sidelined as a minority. Along with some reform-minded nobles and churchmen, they demanded a more democratic, constitutional monarchy. The king, however, despite his frequent hesitations, was firmly committed to maintaining the privileges of the aristocracy and church. He could yield on making taxation fairer, on having an elected assembly with some power, but not on overturning the old order of hereditary statuses.

Frustrated, the Third Estate met on its own in the palace's indoor tennis court on June 20 and constituted itself as a National Assembly.

News of this reached nearby Paris where in July—because of high bread prices, shortages, and a sense that the monarchy wanted to crush reform—rioting and insurrection broke out. This resulted in what became the celebrated event of July 14, the bloody seizure of the royal prison in Paris, the Bastille.

As news of all this spread throughout the countryside in late July and early August, wild rumors began to circulate (what today we might call paranoid fake news). Nobles were said to be plotting with foreigners to intervene and reimpose old feudal dues, or to just let loose roving bandits and looters. Named the "Great Fear," this unleashed the burning of castles and in some cases lynching of nobles.

The Parisian and rural uprisings ensured the Third Estate's triumph by forcing the hand of the royal court and pushing the Third Estate to abolish all so-called feudal (many were not really that ancient) remnants and dues from August 4 to 11. The liberal Declaration of the Rights of Man was passed on August 26. But the continuing unrest in Paris led to an October mass protest march on Versailles led by the city's market women. Upon reaching Versailles, the crowds obliged the threatened court and new National Assembly to move to Paris where the city's radical population could make its power felt more directly.[10]

The revolution quieted down as the hard work of passing reforms and setting up a new kind of constitutional monarchy got under way in the newly constituted National Constituent Assembly. But the ostensible stabilizing success of moderate Enlightenment liberalism from late 1789 to 1791 began to disintegrate. The turn against the church provoked deep division within France. The king, feeling virtually imprisoned in the Tuileries Palace in Paris and unwilling to give in to all the demands for reducing his powers, tried to flee with his family to join troops being assembled on France's borders to intervene in his favor. In a dramatic turning point, the royals got caught on June 20–21, 1791, and were brought back to Paris. The radical forces claimed the attempted flight appeared to prove there was a mounting threat of war because the royalists were plotting with European monarchies, especially Austria, to intervene. This was exacerbated by the popular disdain for the queen, Marie-Antoinette, who was considered extravagantly wasteful and, furthermore, treacherous, as she was an Austrian member of the Habsburg Empire's ruling family. The radicals were invigorated as the moderates faced the bleak prospect of dealing with an intransigent, possibly treacherous king and queen. Major liberal leaders such as Condorcet and the marquis de La Fayette were sidelined because they were still hoping to create a constitutional monarchy.[11]

Why was a National Assembly dominated by progressive, reformist nobles and bourgeois imbued with Enlightenment liberalism unsuccessful in keeping itself in power? For one thing, compared to their American counterparts who had also been inspired by the Enlightenment, most of them had not had much governing experience and had no established parliamentary institutions to use.

The American Revolution's main leaders had more than a theoretical understanding of parliamentary politics and were mostly members of the elites who had played prominent roles in the colonies' governing institutions. The young Alexander Hamilton came from a different background, but during the revolution his political patron was George Washington, who was very much a part of that elite. Rather than abandoning the parliamentary institutions that had been active in the colonies, they used them as the basis for a new union. Then, also, the Americans did not have to deal with an unruly, radicalized big urban center like Paris. Finally, and perhaps just as crucially, the American Revolution never took an anti-Christian turn because there was no rich, reactionary, powerful official church against which to revolt. That the French Revolution had to deal with a politically and economically very powerful church that defended traditional institutions created a deep split in the society. Counterrevolutionary rebellion by the most Catholic parts of France was responsible for the worst of the civil war that convulsed France during the revolution. In other words, the American Revolution was not nearly as socially or cultural radical as the French one, and its more moderate leaders did not face the challenges that destroyed their French counterparts.[12]

There is something particularly tragic in the career of Condorcet, who devised interesting rules and proposals to make democracy work while not really understanding how unpractical this was in the face of popular anger and radicalism. Equally sad was the career of La Fayette, who at first was very popular but lost control of his troops. His reasoned defense of constitutional monarchy was completely undermined by the royal court's obstinacy and Louis XVI's attempted flight.[13]

To head off what was assumed to be an impending invasion to overthrow the revolution and put the monarchy back in power, France declared war against Austria and Prussia in April and June of 1792, and eventually against most other European powers. At first the war went badly. The more extreme revolutionaries, the Jacobins, whose leaders included the lawyer Maximilien Robespierre and the popular radical journalist Jean-Paul Marat, were backed by the Parisian population that blamed the generals and the royals for these defeats. There was rioting in Paris by the *sans-culottes* (the common people, whose men wore long trousers instead of the knee breeches—*culottes*—of the nobles and rich bourgeois). Robespierre's philosophical model was Jean-Jacques Rousseau; he was inspired by Rousseau's message that real democracy meant rule by the collective will of the masses, though it was never clear in Rousseau or his many later radical followers exactly how that was to be institutionalized.

The overprinting of the revolution's new money, the *assignats*, had resulted in inflation, and the peasants were refusing to sell their produce for this debased currency, so there were food shortages and high prices in the cities. France's richest slave colony, Haiti, was in revolt, and some food imports from the Caribbean were no longer arriving.

Order was restored, but in July militias from outside the city, the *fédérés*, stormed into Paris. The contingent from Marseille arrived singing the new revolutionary song, "La Marseillaise." This bloodcurdling war song that would become the French national anthem called on all citizens to rally against the nation's domestic and foreign enemies to exterminate them.

The moderate constitutionalists had lost control. On August 10 the provincial *fédérés* and their *sans-culottes* Parisian allies invaded the Tuileries Palace. The king's Swiss Guards opened fire and some four hundred in the crowd were killed, but the crowd overcame the guards and slaughtered them. The royal family was imprisoned.[14]

On August 19 La Fayette fled. He would then be imprisoned for five years by the Austrians and later, as an old man, would come to play an important role in French politics once more in 1830. Had he and his allies remained in power, the revolution, and modern European history, would have taken a very different and more benign turn.[15]

The Rise of the Bolsheviks

The French Revolution of 1789 was unexpected. The February 1917 Russian one was far less of a surprise. Russia's autocratic monarchy had been under attack by revolutionaries for decades. The well-educated intelligentsia, including many professionals, students, and important officials, knew that the tsarist autocracy was an increasingly dysfunctional anachronism. Much of the growing middle class had been losing faith in the government's conduct of World War I. This was true even of many in the privileged yet disaffected nobility, who no longer trusted the absolute monarch, Tsar Nicholas II. Though reforms had occurred in the countryside, most of the peasants were still technologically backward and very poor. Peasants constituted over 80 percent of the population, and the army consisted largely of conscripted peasant men. Since about 1890 Russian industry had grown at a tremendously rapid rate, producing a new urban working class that was poorly paid and had few rights. Finally, the enormous Russian Empire contained many minorities, some of whom, like the Jews, were relegated to second-class citizenship and suffered episodes of persecution. Many others—Finns, Balts, Ukrainians, Muslims in Central Asia, and people in the Caucasus— were becoming nationalists who questioned the right of Russia to rule them. In the early twentieth century Russia was the least modernized of the European great powers, and the world war's disasters made the situation far worse because it was eating up so many resources and so much manpower. By late 1916 Russia was in much more dire straits than France had been just before its revolution.

There were, however, some startling similarities between these two cases. Louis XVI and Nicholas II were far too powerful given the complexity of the problems they faced, especially as neither was particularly competent or able to overcome the prejudices that had been inculcated in them during their conservative, religious educations. They were both stubbornly resistant to reforms that might undermine their claims to absolute, God-given power. They barely understood how much change there had been in their modernizing societies. The classes that should have been their main source of support—the landowning nobility, the administrative echelons, and, in the case of Russia, also the new business bourgeoisie—had lost faith in antiquated monarchical institutions. After the French and Russian revolutions these unhappy upper and middle classes found out that the fall of their monarchies had put them in mortal danger, but by then it was too late to go back.

Few other twentieth-century revolutionary situations shared quite the same antecedents of having overly powerful monarchs who just could not understand or adapt to the problems their modernizing societies faced. There was, however, one very similar case, the Iranian Revolution of 1979. The shah of Iran, a vain man of limited capacity, installed and then kept in power by British and American interests that originally treated him as a mere figurehead, had become far too powerful. Iran also lacked, as France did in 1789 and Russia in 1917, strong supporting institutions that could have better represented, understood, and dealt with the frustrations of both elites and the masses in a rapidly changing environment. Furthermore, Iran's shah was also no longer viewed as legitimately entitled to hold on to such absolute power, as had been the case for the French and Russian monarchies. (There will be more on Iran below.)[16]

In 1905 the Russian monarchy had come close to being overthrown by an uprising provoked by its incompetent management of the Russo-Japanese War and real hardships endured by the working class and peasantry. When peaceful protesters were fired upon in the capital, St. Petersburg, on January 9, 1905, hundreds died or were wounded, and revolution broke out. (Dates provided here are based on the Julian calendar, which was thirteen days behind the Gregorian, more widely used modern calendar. Russia adopted the Gregorian calendar only in 1918 after the Bolsheviks took power, so until then add thirteen days to each Russian date.) Repression combined with some limited political reforms allowed the regime to survive at the price of granting a kind of constitutional system that was supposed to curb the power of the tsar; but subsequently Nicholas and his advisers were able to neuter the new parliament, the Duma. Then, increasingly, the royal family, Nicholas and Empress Alexandra, fell under the sway of a charismatic but very corrupt monk, Rasputin, who seemed able to control their son and heir's hemophilia. That a peasant monk who was obviously dissolute had become so powerful alienated even the most loyal members of the elite.

There were reforms and both economic and social progress led by the tsar's best ministers, Sergei Witte and Pyotr Stolypin. But the tsar and much of the court bureaucracy were suspicious and resisted change. Witte was sidelined, and the even more reformist and dynamic Stolypin was assassinated in 1911 by an agent of the tsarist secret police, the Okhrana. (There is, however, no evidence that the Okhrana itself was directly involved.) The peasants had been freed from serfdom in 1861, but they had remained bound to the land by traditional communal control of property and by debts. This made it difficult to develop a more progressive, entrepreneurial class of small landowners. Stolypin's reforms privatized property in the hope that this would create such a class. Stolypin knew that rapid industrialization would modernize Russia, but that the country needed stability and peace for at least twenty years to make good progress. To obtain those decades of quiet, he believed it necessary to play down the Russian nationalism that exacerbated tensions with Germany and Austria-Hungary, had led to the disastrous war against Japan, and was antagonizing the non-Russian minorities within the empire.[17]

Neither Stolypin's wish for peace nor Rasputin's entirely rational plea to the tsar in 1914 to avoid war succeeded in warding off the catastrophe that ensued.

In response to Austria-Hungary's declaration of war against Russia's ally Serbia on July 15, 1914—the outcome of the June assassination of Archduke Ferdinand and his wife in Sarajevo on June 15—Nicholas called for Russia to fully mobilize its army on July 17–18. Germany, Austria-Hungary's supporter and enabler, then declared war on Russia on July 19. (Remember, for the rest of the world this was August 1.) France, Russia's ally, mobilized in order to be prepared for what it feared would be a German invasion—an invasion that in fact did materialize two days later. Part of Germany's plan was to immediately invade Belgium on the way to France, so Great Britain felt obliged to declare war against Germany the next day to honor its pledge to help France resist German aggression. World War I was under way.[18]

In 1913, the marginalized revolutionary leader of a small Bolshevik party, Vladimir Ilyich Lenin, had despaired that after three centuries of rule the tsarist Romanov family hardly seemed likely to lose power. He had been living for many years in Switzerland and feared he would never get back. He wrote, "A war between Austria and Russia would be a very useful thing for the revolution, but it is not likely that Franz Joseph [emperor of Austria-Hungary] and Nikolasha [Tsar Nicholas II] will give us that pleasure."[19] But they did.

Despite a surge of Russian patriotism at the start of the war, and the great size of its army, Russia was not prepared to face the more technologically advanced, better led, and more disciplined German army, though it could match the Austro-Hungarians. The Russian army was not as hopeless as the common overwrought simplifications suggest, and, after all, both the French and German armies eventually also suffered serious problems sustaining this terrible war. For Austria-Hungary the war was as much of a disaster as it was for Russia. But that said, the Russians did suffer immense casualties, and the economy could not withstand the strains of a long-term war. In September 1915 Tsar Nicholas made the stupid decision to take personal charge of the army. He moved to the army's headquarters on the Western Front, leaving Petrograd (the capital, St. Petersburg, renamed to sound more Russian) for long periods of time. Too much of the running of affairs was left to Empress Alexandra, who was influenced by Rasputin. As the situation deteriorated, with German advances and ever-greater Russian casualties, public opinion inclined to the view that Alexandra, who had been born a German, and Rasputin were actually German agents betraying Russia (mirroring denunciations of the French queen, Marie-Antoinette, as an "Austrian traitor"). In fact, this was false and Alexandra hated her husband's cousin Kaiser Wilhelm II, but the growing disasters and protests in 1916 against the war were real enough.[20] Rasputin was murdered by a conspiracy of high nobles on December 17, 1916. It was too late, and the elimination of Rasputin did nothing to solve Russia's problems other than to further delegitimize the royal family.

By January 1917 the situation in Petrograd was becoming dire. There were frequent strikes by its now-large industrial workforce of over four hundred thousand, the military and police units protecting the capital were unreliable, and the ministers in charge of the Interior (including the police) and War departments were notoriously incompetent, corrupt appointees who had been instated by Rasputin. There had been a serious uprising in Muslim Central Asia in 1916, and unrest among peasants against the draft.

Though Lenin's Bolsheviks were slowly gaining followers among industrial workers, at the start of 1917 they had only about twenty-four thousand members, and most of the Bolshevik leaders were in exile elsewhere in Europe or under loose detention in Siberia.[21]

As the strikes and protests intensified, and troops mingled with the angry crowds, calls grew from liberal and socialist opposition parties for a thorough cleansing and reform of the government. Lenin's Bolsheviks, it should be noted, were still minor actors at this point, and not, as Soviet historiography would later claim, the main leaders. On February 23 the protests greatly increased. On the 26th some troops fired on the protesters, killing many, and on the 27th the government collapsed. Two institutions claiming power emerged, a Provisional Government in the Duma, the previously partly marginalized parliament, and a Petrograd Soviet (council) of workers and mutinous soldiers and sailors. The former was led by previously well-known liberals, mostly in the Constitutional Democratic Party ("Kadet" for short). At its heart were professionals and intellectuals who had been in the opposition within the Duma until 1917. The Kadets might earlier have been a reformist governing party had the tsar been willing to allow this. The Petrograd Soviet was led by more radical social democrats, the Mensheviks and the SRs (Socialist Revolutionaries). The Mensheviks were one of two factions that had emerged from the split of the Russian Social Democrats in 1903. The other faction comprised the much less numerous (despite its claim to being the majority of the Social Democrats) Bolsheviks led by Lenin. The SRs had widespread peasant support, while the Mensheviks were a main group supported by the workers, soldiers, and sailors.

Faced by the unwillingness of his soldiers and police to support him, Nicholas II was forced to abdicate on March 2 while on his way back to Petrograd from his military headquarters. A brief effort to get one of his brothers to take the throne failed, as Grand Duke Michael refused. The monarchy was dead.[22]

World War I was still closely contested, and Germany hoped to push Russia out in order to move a large part of its eastern armies to the Western Front against the French and British, especially since the United States was obviously moving toward joining and could provide enough manpower and resources to tip the balance. A quick victory in the west was necessary. The Germans then made a fateful decision that would reshape the twentieth century in a way that was at the time completely unforeseen. Lenin had already been known to the German officials as a fiercely antiwar revolutionary. In 1915 he had promulgated a doctrine of "revolutionary defeatism" that would allow revolution to break out in response to war losses. After learning of the overthrow of the monarchy, Lenin used intermediaries to contact the German government about helping him get through Germany, back to Russia where he could speed Russia's exit from the war. On March 23 the Germans appropriated five million gold marks (about a million US dollars at that time, or roughly twenty to twenty-five million today) to promote revolution in Russia, and on March 27 Lenin and a small entourage boarded a train in Switzerland that would take them through Germany and then by ferry to neutral Sweden. They would finish the trip by sled to Russian-held Finland, and finally by train to Petrograd, where they arrived at the Finland Railway Station on April 3. Lenin immediately and publicly demanded "all power to the Soviets," abolition of the Russian army, and withdrawal from the war. This was such an extreme position that even among his Bolshevik supporters there was considerable hesitation, and of course the existing Duma-led government had no such intention. But Lenin had made his point.

This was not, however, the end of German involvement. Money continued to be funneled to Lenin to pay for printing Bolshevik propaganda and even to hand out to potential followers. It is not that this funding was necessarily decisive, but it did permit the Bolsheviks to spread their message to workers, soldiers, and sailors in the Baltic fleet quartered on the nearby island of Kronstadt. As long as the war and shortages continued, Lenin's message gradually gained credence.[23]

The new, mostly liberal Duma-led Provisional Government, however, was unable to assert its authority because it neither ended the war nor proved able to command the resources to relieve economic hardship. Its strongest official, minister of war Alexander Kerensky, was a brilliant orator and believer in a moderate form of socialism, but he also thought that Russia should stay in the war and go on the offensive to save its honor, regain lost territory, and generally raise troop morale. In July that offensive failed badly, resulting in another two hundred thousand Russian casualties and the disintegration of troop morale that made further offensives impossible. That Kerensky thought an offensive could succeed is testimony to his incomprehension about the reality of the situation. On the other hand, most liberals and more moderate socialists supported him, unlike Lenin's Bolsheviks.

From July 3 to 7 there was an attempted uprising in Petrograd that the Bolsheviks tried to lead against the Provisional Government, but it was successfully repressed. An order was issued to arrest leading Bolsheviks, and Lenin, shorn of his beard and wearing a wig, fled. Kerensky, despite his failures, remained the strongest member of the government and became its prime minister on July 11.[24]

Then came the final Kerensky blunder, the mishandling of the so-called Kornilov affair. General Lavr Kornilov had been appointed commander of Russian forces by Kerensky when he became prime minister. In late August, Kornilov assembled forces to march on Petrograd and suppress the Petrograd Soviet. By this time, Bolshevik influence had grown significantly in the Soviet, as they were the firmest opponents of continuing the war and pushed for the dismantling of the traditional army's discipline. Kerensky panicked and agreed to have the workers who supported the Petrograd Soviet armed to form "Red Guard" units against Kornilov, and Bolshevik leaders were freed. Railway workers blocked the trains, agitators convinced the troops to abandon Kornilov, and the march on Petrograd fizzled. Disgruntled soldiers who did not want to be sent back to the front rallied against the army, as did the already-revolutionary sailors based at the nearby Kronstadt naval base. The anti-Bolshevik and antirevolutionary right never forgave Kerensky, whom they accused of having betrayed Kornilov. But the left accused Kerensky of having originally conspired with Kornilov, so by the end of this fiasco on August 27 Kerensky had lost support on both the right and the left.[25] It was a strangely familiar replication of what had happened to La Fayette. By September, the Bolsheviks had gained majorities in the Petrograd and Moscow Soviets and had as allies the left wing of the Socialist Revolutionaries. They thus had the support of hundreds of thousands of workers, and also the passive acquiescence of the peasants who supported the SRs and believed the left's promise to let them keep the land they had spontaneously seized from landlords.[26]

With the Provisional Government in near collapse, on October 25 the Bolsheviks took over Petrograd with their armed supporters, and on the next day they stormed the former tsar's Winter Palace where the remnants of the Provisional Government were entrenched. Though this action was later dramatized by Bolshevik propaganda, and especially by Sergei Eisenstein's brilliant film fabrication, *October: Ten Days That Shook the World*, there was in fact very little fighting, as the members of the government fled without putting up resistance. The Bolsheviks were still allied to the larger left SRs, but they controlled the Petrograd and soon after the Moscow Soviets. Lenin and his brilliant, arrogant second in command, Lev Davidovich Trotsky—who had done even more than Lenin to take control of the Petrograd Soviet—were in charge.

Voting for a new Constituent Assembly took place throughout Russia on November 12 as originally planned. Of the 707 delegates elected, 175 were Bolsheviks (just under 25 percent), 370 were SRs, 40 were Left SRs, 16 were Mensheviks, and 17 were Kadets. The rest represented various regional and ethnic parties. The more moderate socialists, the regular SRs and Mensheviks, therefore had a majority, though in urban industrial parts of Russia the Bolsheviks had obtained a majority of the votes, and in the army about half. Lenin and Trotsky, however, moved quickly to prevent the Constituent Assembly from functioning. On November 23 Kadet and SR members of the All-Russian Commission for Elections were arrested. The assembly met in early January 1918, but the Bolsheviks barred any who opposed them and fired on protesters. The assembly was soon dissolved, and the Bolsheviks were too well organized and armed for any effective resistance to be mounted. Russia would not have another fair general election until the 1990s.[27]

In addition to the similarities between France in 1789 and Russia in 1917, the immediate aftermaths of the two revolutions also had striking parallels. The moderate liberals in both cases had been shut out of power by the prerevolutionary regimes and so had little governing experience. Once they got power, at least briefly, they failed to understand how much popular resentment there was stemming from economic hardship and suspicion of elites by both peasants and urban workers. The liberal notables were seen by the urban radicals as too much a part of the old system. In both cases these elites were far better educated and richer than the general urban and rural populations, and they did not have enough contact with these groups to understand the depth of their hatreds. Then, when more radical leaders took power, in both cases the most extremist ones were willing to turn on liberals and even on former allies who were thought to be too moderate. They did not hesitate to murder as many as necessary to take and hold power. The more moderate forces got the point too late. In Russia in particular the SRs and Mensheviks consistently underestimated Lenin's ruthlessness, though they should have known better, as his writings had long made that clear. In both France and Russia, the incompetence of royal governments and of the liberals who were the first beneficiaries of revolution left the political field open to much more radical forces.

Despite these similarities, there was one crucial difference. Robespierre and his closest associates, like Louis Antoine de Saint-Just, lacked the kind of well-worked-out plan of action and disciplined cadres of followers that the Bolsheviks had built. The Jacobins were not an established party, and they had no coherent theoretical base for their ideology. Lenin, like Trotsky and the rest of the Bolshevik leadership, knew the history of the French Revolution very well, and understood that if they hesitated too much, or failed to take advantage of the situation, they would be overthrown. There were, of course, opponents within the Bolshevik Party to Lenin's extremism, but Lenin's strong reputation as a Marxist thinker and his tenacious insistence on his positions were easily able to overcome them. Unlike Robespierre, Lenin, his second in command Trotsky, and many others, like Nikolai Ivanovich Bukharin, were not only brilliant writers and polemicists, but also excellent political tacticians, and after taking power they seem never to have been as beset by crippling indecision or doubts as Robespierre had been. So they kept the power they had seized.

Another Royal Incompetent and the Rise of
Revolutionary Theocracy in Iran

We have already seen that the Iranian Revolution of 1979 had much in common with the Russian one of 1917. Shah Mohammed Reza Pahlavi, *Shahanshah* ("King of Kings"), was a megalomaniac who thought that by forcing modernization on Iran and spending so many of the billions earned from oil sales on expensive modern arms, he could turn Iran into one of the five great global powers. Almost overthrown in 1953 by a reformist, liberal movement, he had been restored to power by American and British intervention meant to keep Iran's oil in Anglo-American hands. The shah's military, and some of the Shi'a Muslim clerics who were afraid that secular liberals and leftists would weaken their authority, had also turned against the reformist government. Over the next two decades the shah proceeded to severely repress the left and marginalize liberals by his autocratic rule and use of his secret police, SAVAK, known for torturing and murdering opposition figures. Furthermore, he turned against religious leaders who, he felt, retarded progress. Shi'a Muslims make up the large majority of Iranians, and most of the population is devout. Some clerics were imprisoned or exiled, like the esteemed, scholarly Ayatollah Ruhollah Khomeini. (Ayatollahs are major religious theologians recognized as leading teachers.) As religious opposition increased, some of its leaders, including Khomeini's eldest son in 1977, were murdered. The shah's modernization favored the rich, adopted too many Western ways that were offensive to religious Muslims, and, as in other cases of rapid industrialization, pushed vast numbers of peasants and even nomadic tribesmen into urban slums to find work.[28] To top it off, the shah attempted to shift Iranian nationalism away from Islam to ostentatious celebration of a mythologized ancient, pre-Islamic Persian imperial past. Efforts by the liberal, slightly left-of-center National Front to push for democratic reform were also repressed, and the party was made illegal. Many of its leaders, such as Shapour Bakhtiar, were jailed for years at a time.

In response, opposition to the shah, from leftist students, the illegal Communist Party, moderate liberals, religious conservatives, and radical Islamists, covered almost the entire political spectrum. Middle-class merchants threatened by the shah's privileging of large, often Western-owned or -influenced enterprises, also came to be opposed. Even the westernizing new professional middle class, and especially their children who were university students or studying abroad, were outraged by the corruption, the servile acceptance of Western, mostly American influence, and the savage repressive tactics of the regime. Profoundly religious Muslims increasingly loathed the shah's seeming disdain for their faith and his adoption of Western ways.

Despite significant economic growth, by the late 1970s the shah had alienated almost all of Iranian society. While the economy had certainly developed and grown during his reign, glaring, growing inequalities, corruption, and lack of attention to the needs of ordinary peasants and workers created frustrations that were exacerbated by inflation from overspending. The writing of the esteemed, often-persecuted intellectual Ali Shariati, who had tried before his death in 1977 to combine Marxist socialism with Muslim religiosity, was being widely read. But also widely disseminated were the writings and the recorded tapes of Ruhollah Khomeini, who was living in exile, originally in Iraq, but eventually in a suburb of Paris. Whether on the left or the right, among the more religious or the more secular, the excessive aping of Western ways, the support of an interfering America that seemed to unquestionably support the shah, and resentment over the long history of Russian, British, and now American interference in Iranian affairs further delegitimized the monarch.[29]

Throughout 1978 there were an unending series of strikes and demonstrations against the shah that were sometimes brutally repressed with considerable bloodshed. As had happened in revolutionary France and Russia, the shah's army was becoming less reliable because a lot of the ordinary soldiers were unenthusiastic recruits. And as in France in 1788 and Russia in 1916, the monarch was so out of touch with his people that he still thought he was popular, even revered by the masses. It may be correct to say that by early 1978 it would have been possible to reform and avoid a revolution, but that would have required an increasingly delusional shah to change. Furthermore, he was suffering from cancer and was disoriented, and when he finally agreed to reforms after a year of almost constant protests, by late 1978 this was no longer a viable option.

On December 29, 1978, the shah agreed to have Shapour Bakhtiar, the former National Front leader, appointed as prime minister. As with the liberal Kadets in Russia in 1917, that move came too late; moderate reformers had little popular support because they still hoped for a compromise that might have left the monarchy in place. On January 16 at the demand of Bakhtiar, the shah and his family went into what was supposed to be temporary exile. By then, however, it was Ayatollah Khomeini who was seen by most Iranians as the true leader of the revolution because of his uncompromising anti-Westernism, his hostility to the very idea of monarchy, and his deep, learned religiosity. The declining liberals thought they could work with him, and the left, particularly the radical students, saw in Khomeini a figure who would redistribute property and curb both corruption and excessive wealth. Khomeini returned to Iran on February 1, and an estimated five million cheering people lined the streets of Tehran to greet him. Bakhtiar was removed and went into exile in Paris where, in 1991, he was murdered by Iranian agents.

Khomeini was a religious version of Lenin. He was as ideologically inflexible, having long claimed that Iran should be ruled by divine law as interpreted by leading religious judges. In lectures in 1970 under the title *Velayat-e Faqih: Hokumat-e Islami* (The jurist's guardianship: Islamic government), he had argued that all monarchy was un-Islamic and therefore illegitimate. Only a government regulated by pure Shi'a Islamic religious specialists could be legitimate.[30] But like Lenin, he was also tactically shrewd. Iran in 1979 was not ready for quite so radically religious a government, so at first he put religious but more liberal leaders in prominent positions. Only gradually were these leaders eliminated and shoved aside. In 1980 he allowed Abdolhassan Bani Sadr to be elected president. Bani Sadr was a longtime religious dissident, but his theory of government was not as extreme as Khomeini's, and he was gradually sidelined. In 1981 he was impeached. He fled to avoid arrest and went to live in Paris. Khomeini maneuvered to eliminate any resistance to his ideas from several other major ayatollahs, and by 1983 had solidified his rule enough to impose his will such that as supreme religious leader he would have near total power to veto what he thought contrary to Islam.[31]

As in the French and Russian revolutions, where incompetent and outdated royal regimes had resisted moderate reform too long, liberals finally brought to power were unable to satisfy popular demands for greater change; various allies of the radicals naively thought they could control the situation, but turned out to be incapable of doing so.

Before leaving the role of incompetence in the face of crisis, we turn to one different but analogous example, Germany in 1932–1933.

How Incompetent Conservatives Misunderstood Hitler and Doomed Germany

In 1932 Germany faced a terrible situation. The economy had substantially recovered from the disaster of World War I and the inflation of the early 1920s; but after 1929 the Great Depression cast it back into deep crisis. The ill-fated Weimar Republic had never been fully accepted by much of its conservative military and civilian elite, and the Depression also invigorated the far left. The result was the rise of Hitler's Nazi Party, which came increasingly to be seen as a potential savior that could curb the socialist and communist left but also appeal to German nationalism by restoring the nation's strength. Nazism was based on some immense lies: that Germany had lost World War I only because it had been betrayed by Jews and socialists; that Jews controlled the economy and the international system and so kept Germany down; that the Nazi version of racial science proved the inherent superiority of the Germanic, "Aryan" pure race; and that liberal democracy was nothing but a corrupt sham.

Nazism's popular support, however, derived from forces beyond these. Not only did the Nazis promise to end the Depression, but they also appealed to small-town and rural Protestant nostalgia for the lost past and social stability of prewar Germany. These were people shocked by the intellectual, social, and even sexual innovations of sophisticated Weimar Berlin, the most dynamic city in Europe in the 1920s. Nazism thrived among those who felt left behind, not only economically but also socially, by what they perceived to be a degenerate, unpatriotic, cosmopolitan culture. Furthermore, much of this hated culture was perceived to be "foreign," and especially Jewish. The flow of immigrants, mostly Slavs and Jews from the East, was seen as a particular threat. Joseph Goebbels, Hitler's propaganda chief, even promised to build a "wall" against that noxious foreign influx. This was surprisingly similar to the European and American rise of antiliberal populism today, as is so ably brought out in the new analysis of Hitler's rise to power by Benjamin Carter Hett.[32]

The aged president, Paul von Hindenburg, Germany's foremost World War I hero, was a conservative who was nostalgic about the fallen monarchy, but he also despised Adolf Hitler. In the 1932 elections, however, the Nazis became the leading party with a plurality in the Reichstag. Hindenburg was surrounded by reactionary hangers-on who thought they could use the Nazis' popularity while controlling Hitler, and they pressured the ailing eighty-four-year-old president to appoint Hitler as chancellor in January 1933.

Chief among those who maneuvered Hindenburg into putting Hitler in power were his son Oskar (beware of incompetent relatives too close to power!), the president's longtime confidant, Franz von Papen, and the president's chief of staff, Otto Meissner. Von Papen had himself appointed vice-chancellor, confident that he could surround Hitler with trusted conservatives who would hold the Nazis in check. He was totally wrong. Not only had he misunderstood how skilled Hitler was and what kind of drastic radicalism the Nazis stood for; he had also overestimated his own shrewdness. In fact, most German conservatives among its aristocrats, its army officers, and its leading businessmen, and many of its intellectuals, judges, and civil servants were quite willing to go along with the Nazis in the belief that it was worth accepting the party's more extreme racism and autocratic ways in order to bring the left under control and restore Germany to its rightful place.

Hitler's rise to power depended on a set of fortuitous events including the failed attempt by Chancellor Heinrich Brüning (1930–1932) to control the Depression with the sort of deflationary "belt-tightening" policy that also characterized Herbert Hoover's approach to the Depression in the United States. Next came inept leadership by the military's choice for chancellor, the scheming General Kurt von Schleicher, who was unable to find a political solution to parliamentary paralysis. Hindenburg then turned to von Papen, who, however, was equally unable either to win popular approval or to find a workable remedy for Germany's problems. Only after that failure did the plot emerge to put Hitler in power as a figurehead with mass support. The Nazi Party had enthusiastic mass appeal, but it was still far from being supported by the majority of Germans. Once in power, however, the Nazis proceeded to make short work of their opponents on the left, and then purged many of their former allies on the right to gain total control. Hitler's rise to power was the result of naïveté—not that of liberals but that of frustrated conservatives who could not arouse sufficient mass backing for their program and fooled themselves into thinking that they could make Hitler their puppet.[33]

Benito Mussolini had come to power in much the same way in 1922. Fearful conservatives backed by the king of Italy had believed that the Fascist Party could control the left and preserve elite power even if his popular support was less than Mussolini claimed. It took Mussolini much longer to establish total power than it did Hitler, but eventually he succeeded and, like Hitler, proved to have transformative ambitions that eventually drove his country to a ruin that the complaisant conservatives and the monarch had never anticipated.[34]

There is no denying that there were long-standing social, political, economic, and intellectual trends in Germany and Italy that made the rise of fascism possible. Without an understanding of that background, it is impossible to explain how Hitler and Mussolini came to power. The same is true if we want to understand the French, Russian, and Iranian revolutions' turn to extremism. But if prerevolutionary conditions and trends made such outcomes possible, they certainly did not make them inevitable. What needs to be highlighted is the unplanned, unforeseen, and fortuitous events that made previously unknown or, at best, minor or marginalized extremist leaders rise to the top. To add to our understanding, it is also necessary to recognize the role in the trajectory to disaster played by many influential, powerful leaders. These leaders, through their ineptitude and mistakes, failed to adapt to crisis or just misunderstood what was going on. The lack of awareness of the dangers at hand contributed mightily to ultimately drastic revolutionary outcomes.

There is, therefore, a pattern. One of the key errors made in all the cases highlighted so far is the belief that radical revolutionaries who wanted to reshape their societies could easily be controlled by more numerous and ostensibly more powerful moderates on the left or the right. It had happened during the French Revolution, and again with the Bolshevik takeover in Russia. It is what happened as well in Iran in the 1970s and certainly in Germany in the 1930s. Once in power, determined extremists are more than willing to repress and murder those who stand in their way, and so undo the vain hopes of the more moderate forces that helped their ascent before being betrayed.

Radical seizure of power is hardly the end of the process that leads to tragic outcomes. The next step is that extremist revolutionaries use the real or exaggerated threat of counterrevolution and outside intervention to consolidate their power.

3

Reaction, War, Invasion, and Revolutionary Terror

What is this Thing called *La Révolution*, which, like an Angel of Death, hangs over France . . . ? It is the Madness that dwells in the hearts of men . . . as a rage or as a terror, it is in all men.

—THOMAS CARLYLE[1]

Revolutionary war is an antitoxin which not only eliminates the enemy's poison but also purges us of our own filth.

—MAO ZEDONG[2]

REVOLUTIONS WITHOUT OPPONENTS must not be revolutions at all. However many benefits a revolution promises, there are surely some who had benefited from the old regime who will resist. There are others who might begin as neutral or as supporters but quickly discover that the anticipated changes are going to hurt their security and ideals. While foreign intervention is not guaranteed, it is more likely if some outside powers find the revolutions threatening to their interests, or perhaps just see them as an opportunity to take advantage of a country weakened by the resulting chaos.

The American Revolution was opposed by a substantial number of loyalists who wanted to remain British. Tens of thousands fled to other parts of the British Empire after their side lost.[3] As in all anticolonial revolutions, in America's the colonial power came to be viewed as a foreign entity that had no right to rule. But compared to the ferocity of the counterrevolutions and killing involved in later major revolutions, the American Revolution was relatively mild.

The repressions of even potential—or sometimes just imagined and falsely accused—counterrevolutionaries in France, Russia, and later Iran were very bloody. In France the revolution led not only to civil war but also to foreign intervention and a long series of international wars. In Russia outside involvement contributed to a prolonged, terrible civil war. In Iran the very costly Iraqi invasion of 1980 and subsequent eight-year war also exacted a high price in lives. The paradox is that outside intervention and civil war actually strengthened the revolutionaries in all three of these cases and significantly contributed to their radicalization.

The French Reign of Terror: A Model and Lesson for Later Revolutionaries

Overthrowing the monarchy that had survived until 1792 did not at first help the war effort against Austria and Prussia. By September, with a growing number of armed exiles in a counterrevolutionary army on the Austrian border (in what is now Belgium), there was panic in Paris. It was the sense that the moderates were unable to handle the crisis that opened the way for radicals to take over, as they promised to use more drastic means to save the revolution. In early September jailed political prisoners, but also many common-law inmates, in Paris and other cities were massacred by the revolutionaries. Georges Jacques Danton, a lawyer who was one of the radical leaders and was then minister of justice, did not intervene and ever since has been blamed by his detractors for this bloody turn of events.[4]

On September 20, 1792, a new "National Convention," elected by what was supposed to be universal male suffrage but was in reality only about an eighth of that, replaced the Legislative Assembly. The convention cemented the radicals in power. They abolished the monarchy and church privileges as France's First Republic was declared. France was to become a secular state and divorce was legalized, two reforms that went directly against the Catholic Church's prior monopoly on matters of faith and family. Those priests who refused to accept control by the state were persecuted, and forced recruitment of soldiers into the army also began. This mass conscription, the *levée en masse*, swelled the ranks of the French armies, which then greatly outnumbered the prevailing professional and mercenary armies used by the other European powers, but it also provoked counterrevolutionary outbreaks in parts of France that were opposed to the draft. Civil war broke out, most seriously in the Vendée and adjoining parts of western France, where ultimately, after years of conflict, between 250,000 and 300,000 people would perish. Villages were burned and mass killings occurred in attacks, reprisals, and counterreprisals by both sides.[5]

By 1793 the larger French armies of the revolution started to win important victories and restore order in most of France. Two important counterrevolutionary cities, Lyon and Toulon, were subdued. In Toulon the British Mediterranean fleet had come to help the antirevolutionary rebels, and it was there that a young artillery officer fighting with the revolution, Napoleon Bonaparte, first came to prominence by positioning artillery to force out the British fleet. In Lyon the revolutionary forces began mass executions of supposed counterrevolutionaries. A revolutionary policeman, Joseph Fouché, who had once been a priest, was brought from the Vendée, where he had led executions, to do the same in Lyon. He would later play an important role as Napoleon's chief policeman, who inaugurated the modern model of a ruthless secret police.[6]

As the radical Jacobins who had taken control during the 1792 emergency solidified their rule, they had Louis XVI beheaded in January of 1793. His wife, Marie-Antoinette, was guillotined in October. Their son, who would have been Louis XVII, was abused and died at the age of ten in 1795, though he remained a symbol to be revered by sympathizers of the monarchy into the twenty-first century.[7]

The radicals led by the provincial lawyer Maximilien Robespierre began to attack the slightly more moderate supporters of the revolution in a growing Reign of Terror. Those who would eventually be called

Girondistes and had been part of the radical alliance with the Jacobins, but who, for tactical reasons, counseled more moderation, were targeted in a series of dishonest show trials followed by executions. Just being suspected of lack of enthusiasm about the revolution or not fully backing its increasing push to de-Christianize France could lead to accusations of treachery, as happened to Condorcet among many others. A new, anti-Christian calendar was later inaugurated to end Catholic holidays and traditional saints' days. The year 1793 was declared to be year I. (This calendar was ended by Napoleon in 1805 when France reverted to the traditional version. It was briefly revived under the Paris Commune of 1871.)

The Girondistes long afterward in the nineteenth century became heroes of middle-of-the-road liberals who approved of the early but not the radical part of the revolution. Later Marxist historians tried to prove that the Girondistes were actually members of the high bourgeoisie, and their Jacobin enemies were from the small bourgeoisie, but careful analysis has shown that there were few if any class differences between the two groups, which were themselves internally divided. Both were dominated by aspiring professionals, many of them lawyers, whose advancement had been blocked under the old regime because they were not nobles, and both had been behind most radical revolutionary measures until then.[8]

As so often has happened in revolutions, the radicals then began to turn on each other. Robespierre had his onetime friend and collaborator Danton tried and guillotined in 1794 for corruption and betrayal of the revolution. Danton was somewhat corrupt, as were many others, but not Robespierre. As we know, that kind of excuse—corruption—is often manufactured as part of a raw struggle for power, which is what this was about. As for his betrayal, for tactical reasons Danton had also started to question all the bloodshed. Danton would subsequently become a hero of liberals who saw in him a moderate opponent of Robespierre's extremism, but that is a considerable exaggeration. It was particularly in the late nineteenth century, during the liberal Third French Republic, that Danton became an official hero. Glorifying him was meant to save the revolution's liberal side while condemning the

Terror's radicalism. There is a large statue of Danton as a heroic defender of liberty in the heart of Paris, but none of Robespierre.[9]

Much later something similar would happen when leftists glorified Nikolai Bukharin, one of the most important of Lenin's associates. Bukharin was a supporter of radical repression to keep the Bolsheviks in power and, after Lenin's death, a strong Stalin backer. But Bukharin was opposed to Stalin's brutal collectivization of the peasants after 1928 because he feared, correctly, that it would damage Soviet agriculture and bring about unnecessary hardships. He was pushed out of power in 1929 and eventually arrested in 1937. Despite having been one of Stalin's main supporters and presumably a friend, Stalin had him shot in 1938 after a ludicrously mendacious trial. Bukharin was posthumously rehabilitated and accepted as a heroic figure by Mikhail Gorbachev in 1988 as part of the effort to liberalize Soviet Communism while saving its socialist ideals, but by 1988 it was too late.[10] (There will be much more about this below in sections of the book about Russia.)

To return to France, why was there this turn toward revolutionary extremism in France in 1793? Partly it was to satisfy the population of Paris, and other mostly urban constituencies, who wanted revenge for their past sufferings and who despised the old aristocracy. There was also an ever-present fear that foreign intervention and counterrevolutionary nobles, working with the recalcitrant Catholic Church, might use divisions among Republicans to overthrow the revolution. As might be expected, there were not only some ideological differences but also personal rivalries and dislikes among the revolutionary leaders themselves. In the increasingly fevered atmosphere of the period, purges were an obvious way for those with power to get rid of real, presumed, and eventually merely potential enemies.

Finally, in the summer of 1794, after the Terror had resulted in the death of Danton and other former revolutionary notables, as well as tens of thousands of others, frightened members of the republic's parliament, the Convention, reacted before it was too late. They deposed Robespierre and his chief follower, Saint-Just, on July 27 and had them guillotined the next day. In the new revolutionary calendar that had started with year I in 1793, and had replaced the names of the month with ones related to the seasons, the overthrow of the extremists took place on Thermidor 9 (the month of heat), year II. This has been enshrined in historical memory as the "Thermidorian reaction," a return to some moderation after extreme radicalism. The same eventually seems to have happened to other subsequent radical revolutions, but with more delay.[11]

Robespierre, however, later became the hero of the French far left, and eventually of communists everywhere. The pro-communist historian Albert Mathiez (who followed his teacher François-Alphonse Aulard as holder of the University Chair on the Revolution, but moved much further left than his mentor after World War I) wrote in 1922:

> What tragic irony! Robespierre and his party went to their death largely for having tried to use the Terror as the instrument of a fresh upheaval affecting property. With them the leveling Republic, without rich or poor, which they had dreamt of establishing . . . received its death blow.[12]

This is also, if not entirely a fabrication, a great exaggeration. Portrayals of Robespierre as a prototypical Leninist, either by the far left as a hero or, conversely, by the political center and right as an evil fanatic, became part of latter-day political mythology, just as did celebrations of Danton as a benign liberal. Such stories reveal more about the political ideology of those who tell them than about the original historical reality. Robespierre never had the absolute power of a Mao or a Stalin, or the clear ideological vision of Lenin and Trotsky. But he did become a paranoid, power-hungry potential dictator who overestimated his popular support and was responsible for many thousands of unnecessary deaths. In so doing he twisted the revolution into a debacle far removed from the intentions of its original liberal leaders, such as Mirabeau, Sieyès, Condorcet, or La Fayette.[13]

After Thermidor there was a reaction, a host of executions of radicals, and a turn toward a different, more moderate kind of revolution. Far too much had changed to permit restoration of the old regime, but the radical revolution had failed, just as the earlier liberal one had, and what followed was different.

Later the Bolshevik leaders who took over the Russian Revolution understood the danger of a Thermidorian reaction and were determined not to let that happen to them. In some sense it did, but only much later, partly after Stalin's death in 1953, and more drastically in the late 1980s, under Gorbachev, seven decades after 1917.

Civil War and the Creation of
a Terrorizing State in Russia

Lenin had never thought that a successful radical revolution could be gently liberal and avoid serious violence. It turned out, however, that to succeed it had to be even more brutal than he or most of his followers had anticipated, because they had expected more spontaneous support as they enacted decrees to abolish capitalism, distribute land, and give more direct power to workers. They had also hoped that revolutions would break out in Central Europe, especially Germany, so that foreign threats to their regime would be reduced. As it quickly became obvious that these hopes would not materialize, and that resistance to Bolshevism was going to be extremely dangerous, a large coercive apparatus had to be constructed to keep power. This machinery, once created, would become available for future use to fulfill further Bolshevik goals by force. Lenin died in 1924. His successor, Iosif (Joseph) Vissarionovich Stalin, further expanded the institutions of terror to control the population and pursue the Communist Party's ambitious goal of creating a new type of society; but deadly regime terror was already well established while Lenin was still in charge before his first stroke in 1922. By then hundreds of thousands of real and supposed "class enemies" had already been killed and imprisoned.

In December 1917 Lenin set up the Cheka. (Its full name was "All-Russian Extraordinary Commission to Combat Counterrevolution and Sabotage." "Extraordinary Commission" in Russian has the initials ЧК, Che Ka, that gave it its commonly used name.) It was a ruthless enforcement agency created to curb, imprison, torture, and kill enemies. Lenin placed it outside direct control of the government he had established,

Sovnarkom, so that it could operate as a secret police. This later became the GPU, the OGPU, the NKVD, and eventually, after many reorganizations and changes of names, the KGB. Lenin installed "Iron" Felix Dzerzhinsky, a seasoned Polish revolutionary organizer who had already suffered numerous arrests, exiles, and beatings by the tsarist secret police, as its director.[14]

It is extraordinary how many leading revolutionaries, such as Dzerzhinsky, Stalin, and hundreds of others, had been identified by the tsarist secret police, the Okhrana, had been arrested numerous times, had escaped, and had then been recaptured and exiled to Siberia but not killed. Had the tsarist regime, which certainly did not hesitate to be cruel, been as ruthless as the Bolsheviks and slaughtered all such individuals, there might never have been a Bolshevik Revolution at all. Practically all of the early Bolsheviks had suffered, or like Lenin fled into exile, but survived to come to power. Lenin and his associates certainly learned from this, and neither within Russia nor when it came to their worst enemies abroad did the Cheka hesitate to murder. Lenin and his followers were not afraid to order killings on such a scale that inevitably a lot of innocents also died, but gradually all possible opposition was crushed.

At first the new Bolshevik regime tried to stall the German advance into Russia while waiting for revolution to break out among its troops and within Germany itself, but that did not happen. Against much opposition, even within his own party, Lenin pushed through the peace treaty of Brest-Litovsk with the Germans in March 1918. As the Russian army had by then practically disintegrated, the Bolsheviks had little leverage. The treaty gave Germany a virtually free hand to control much of western Russia, including Ukraine, until Germany had to withdraw when it surrendered to the Western Allies in November 1918. Lenin proved to have been right to be so accommodating. Ending the war against Germany gave the Bolsheviks some popularity and, especially, time to consolidate their rule.

The revolutionary regime faced many threats. The Bolsheviks had distrusted the traditional army and thought they might rely on popular militias to defend themselves from domestic and foreign enemies, but that was also unrealistic. The Cheka was crucial, but not sufficient. A real army had to be constructed.

Leon Trotsky took on the task and proved to be brilliant. He insisted, against much party opposition, that former tsarist officers willing to join the new Red Army to defend Russia should be given the opportunity to do so. He also picked able commanders to lead newly formed units. He imposed traditional military training and discipline, and a draft was organized. In this he followed the policies that had made the French Revolution's armies so effective.

Foreign armies intervened against the Russian Revolution, and ethnic minorities—in the Baltic, all along the western borders, among Cossacks, in the Caucasus, and in Central Asia—rebelled. Particularly dangerous were an army led by the former tsarist General Anton Denikin in southern Russia and another in Siberia led by Admiral Alexander Kolchak, who was for a while recognized by some Western powers as the leader of Russia. These forces, the so-called Whites (as opposed to the "Reds") captured much of the land and threatened to get to Moscow. But they never satisfactorily coordinated their activities, and both Denikin and Kolchak refused to promise non-Russian, former imperial territories their independence. They therefore failed to take advantage of strong anticommunist and pro-independence sentiments in the Baltics. They also lost the opportunity to forge an alliance with a newly independent Finland, whose army could have attacked Petrograd and helped General Nikolai Yudenich, who led a White army against that city. Without that help, Yudenich's attack failed. Kolchak's Siberian base had too little access to resources and population, and ultimately did no better. The Bolsheviks who controlled the Russian core managed to hold Petrograd, Moscow, and some other centrally located cities with their industries, large populations, and friendly workers. This gave them the ability to move troops and supplies more easily than could the divided, disparate opposition.

When World War I ended, American, British, French, and Japanese forces remained on Russian territory. There was also a Czech Legion, composed of captured Austrian soldiers from the Austrian provinces

REACTION, WAR, INVASION, TERROR 45

that would become Czechoslovakia. They had been sent across Siberia to the Pacific in order to rejoin the war on the Allied side. They wound up heavily armed but stranded along the Trans-Siberian Railway, where they became a potential source of support for Kolchak's Whites. For a time, they posed a serious anti-Bolshevik threat, but eventually they left. The Red Army let them go unharmed in return for their turning over the defeated Admiral Kolchak. The admiral was promptly shot. The British, French, and Americans were tired of war and never posed that serious a threat, though they certainly provided supplies for the Whites. The Japanese stayed longer in Siberia but eventually left too. Perhaps even more importantly, the Western Allies unwittingly validated Bolshevik propaganda that was able to mobilize Russian antiforeign nationalism against them. The French Revolution had benefited from the same sort of nationalism, and the Iranian Revolution would too. Having a visible foreign enemy always arouses patriotism, no matter what government is in power.

More dangerously, there was a newly resurrected Poland formed after the Great War from territories that had previously been divided among the Austrian, German, and Russian empires. Poland invaded Ukraine in 1920 to set up a state that was to be associated with it, reviving an old claim. Poland had once controlled much of Ukraine before being dismantled by Russia, Austria, and Prussia in the eighteenth century. The Red Army, led by one of its outstandingly brilliant young generals, the twenty-seven-year-old Mikhail Tukhachevsky, came close to overrunning Poland in a counterattack but was then itself beaten back, and a peace treaty was signed between the two states.

By 1921, most of what had been Russia had been reconquered by the Bolsheviks, but the three Baltic countries of Estonia, Latvia, and Lithuania had gained their freedom, as did Finland. Communists in those places were unable to gain a foothold, though they tried. Lenin ultimately knew that it was wiser to give in to them in order to consolidate what his Bolsheviks controlled. On the other hand, under the very able leadership of two young Bolshevik generals in their midthirties, Mikhail Frunze and Vladimir Antonov-Ovseyenko (who had personally led the Bolshevik invasion of the Winter Palace in Petrograd to seize power during the October 1917 Revolution), Ukraine was retaken, and the last of the southern White army, now led by General Baron Wrangel, was pushed out of Crimea, its last redoubt, into exile. Ukrainian independence forces under Symon Petliura and a Ukrainian anarchist army led by Nestor Machno were destroyed.

A very large Russia, now firmly communist, had survived the civil wars and foreign intervention. Ultimately the Central Asian independence movements were defeated, but only after more fighting until 1926. Also defeated were the southern Caucasian independence movements in Azerbaijan, Armenia, and also Georgia, which had been ruled by Mensheviks in its few years of independence from 1918 to 1921. All were reunited in the new Communist Empire called the Union of Soviet Socialist Republics—the USSR, as it was renamed in 1922. It would go on to survive as a great world power until 1991.[15]

Despite these successes, the state of the economy was terrible, and the increasingly repressive nature of Bolshevik rule was creating growing discontent. There were many local peasant uprisings to protest the forcible seizure of their produce in order to feed the army and cities. As the urban centers were the main source of Bolshevik support, the continuing conflict turned into a kind of warfare between the cities and the countryside. The society was still at least 80 percent rural, and the peasants might have seemed to have an advantage, but actually their revolts were scattered, they never united, and they lacked modern weapons, so they were easily defeated. Marxist-Leninist theory had never trusted the peasants, and what happened in the civil war would later be used to justify Stalin's destruction of the peasantry.

In late February of 1921 something even more dangerous occurred. The sailors at the big Kronstadt naval base on an island near Petrograd, once a key center of Bolshevik support, demanded reforms that would democratize Russia and allow genuine benefits for workers. Lenin considered this the most serious threat to the Bolsheviks, worse than the White armies and peasant uprisings. Trotsky ordered the Red Army to suppress the rebellion. At the start of March, General Tukhachevsky, in command of about sixty thousand troops, attacked Kronstadt, crossing the still-frozen sea that separated the base from the mainland. Thousands were killed, and after the rebellion was broken, thousands more were executed or sent to labor camps. The repression of Kronstadt was final proof, if any were needed, that Lenin and his Bolsheviks had no intention of allowing any opposition to prevail, even from those who had once been key supporters.[16]

The civil and international wars had taken a terrible toll, and the institutions the Bolsheviks had created to win had become inured to unlimited brutality in order to survive. Mass slaughters by all sides had occurred. Torture, rape, and widespread looting had ravaged the country. Jews had suffered particularly grievously from pogroms committed by the Whites and Ukrainian independence forces, but also to some extent by the Red Army itself, even though many Bolshevik leaders were secular Jews and in principle such behavior was not approved. Over fifty thousand Jews, and possibly as many as two hundred thousand, had been killed, with more than that injured and raped. The very widespread anti-Semitism throughout Russia needs to be remembered, as it played an important role in subsequent events, though at least through most of the 1920s Jewish Bolsheviks had a disproportionately consequential place in sustaining Communist rule. That would all change in the 1930s.[17]

It was not just the wars that had so badly damaged the economy, but also attempts to impose a rough form of socialism that had been responsible for provoking so much opposition from previously sympathetic parts of the urban and rural populations. Without its repressive apparatus, even after having prevailed in most of its civil wars, Bolshevik rule would have been far more fragile. It is worth getting some sense of how bad things were to explain why Lenin in 1921 proposed to relax socialism and accept some free market reforms. There was no intention to decrease the power of the Communist Party's repressive capacities, but this New Economic Policy (NEP) was meant to restore the economy to health.

How bad was it in 1921? Some ten and a half million had died, roughly three-quarters of them from famine and disease brought on by the civil wars. Within a few more years, up to five million more would die of famine. Two million had gone into permanent exile. This was added to the 3.3 million military and civilian deaths from World War I. A census in 1926 would show that the USSR had 147 million people. Discounting the parts of the Russian Empire lost after 1918, had these catastrophes not occurred, there might instead have been about 170 million people.[18]

By 1921 the Russian economy had lost 70 percent of its industrial production. In 1918 alone as much was lost as during the World War I years 1914–1917, not only because of fighting, but even more because of mismanagement of confiscated enterprises and the sidelining of "bourgeois" managers. Agricultural production by 1921 was 60 percent of what it had been in 1913, and railroad tonnage was only 25 percent of its prewar capacity. Peasants were unwilling to sell their produce for a worthless currency, and efforts to set up collectives by pitting poorer peasants against richer ones in collective arrangements were a dismal failure. Then, as later in the collectivization drive after 1929, the existence of a "kulak" class of rich, exploiting peasants was a figment of Leninist imagination. Provoking conflict in villages did not, therefore, help. On top of all that, until 1920 some of the richest agricultural areas of southern Russia were under White control. All this caused massive unemployment, famine, and disease in the cities. Many died; others fled. By 1920 the population of Petrograd had fallen by two-thirds, from 2,500,000 to about 750,000, and Moscow's had fallen about a third. Only forced confiscations of food by the Red Army and the Cheka managed to keep the regime afloat, though that provoked yet more uprisings and need for repression. It is therefore understandable that Lenin, against some hardline leftist opposition within his party, decided to push forward with the NEP.[19] And indeed, the NEP worked: the economy gradually began to improve.

Despite all these tragedies and hardships, however, growing numbers of young people, enthused by the idea of creating a new type of freer, more democratic, drastically egalitarian society, joined the Communist Party after 1917. There were promises of greater sexual freedom, gender equality, revolutionary high culture, and much else. These new converts provided the cadres of the new institutions, including the army and the Cheka as well as planners, managers, teachers, and others necessary to keep the Communist Party and the Soviet Union functioning. In early

1917, before the revolution, there had been twenty-four thousand members of Lenin's Bolshevik Party. By the end of 1921 there were over seven hundred thousand, most of whom were from worker or peasant backgrounds, who had joined in dangerous times and not just out of opportunism. Many of them remembered this period from 1917 to 1921 as a glorious time of "War Communism." It was a high point in their young lives, to be viewed as a heroic struggle against reactionary, antiprogressive foreign and domestic foes. Had the Bolsheviks simply been power-grabbing hypocrites, as many of their enemies insisted, this would not have been possible. As it was, there was enough of a genuinely idealistic, if ruthless, ruling Communist Party to impose central control and repress local dissent after 1921.[20] Thus, while the relaxation of socialist control of the economy and relative freedom granted by the party during the years of the NEP did bring more personal freedom and the flourishing of an innovative new culture, these changes did not weaken party control or in any sense eliminate the repressive institutions that had been built up.[21]

The memory of the glorious sacrifices and trials of this period would play a major role in making this new generation of communists the base of support for Stalin when he moved to consolidate his power after Lenin's death, and then later, in the 1930s, to purge and kill much of the older, original generation of Bolshevik leaders.

The French Got Napoleon. The Russians Got Stalin. Why Not Trotsky or Tukhachevsky?

After the Thermidorian reaction, the French Revolution had settled down into its First Republic and continued to pass modernizing reforms, but the regime, the Directoire (Directory), was unable to calm the continuing disputes between radical Jacobins and the more moderate revolutionaries. Nor could it bring under complete control still-active royalist sentiments. Furthermore, it remained at war with the other major European powers, who considered the revolution an abomination. From 1794 to 1799, the Directory came to rely ever more on its military, swelled by the draft, to fight off foreign and domestic enemies.

The army itself, with its crop of young, able, revolutionary generals, became a dominant political player. This brought Napoleon Bonaparte to the forefront.

After his successes in forcing the British out of Toulon and regaining that city for the revolution, he was sent to northern Italy where France was fighting Austria. His success there as a brilliant artillery general in 1794 gained him a sterling reputation. In 1795 he further endeared himself to the government by using artillery to put down a royalist uprising in Paris. Sent back to Italy in 1796 as commander of French forces, he defeated the Austrians and their Italian allies, setting up a French protectorate. His popularity was now such that he was becoming a danger. In 1797—partly to get him out of the way, but also to try to secure the Mediterranean and possibly set up a base from which to invade British India—the Directory put Napoleon in charge of a large French expedition to conquer Egypt. Success would avenge France's 1763 loss of India to the British after the Seven Years' War. Napoleon accepted the commission and sailed in 1798.

Egypt was formally part of the Ottoman Empire but actually run by local Mamelukes—an elite Muslim armed force consisting of former slave mercenaries. Napoleon easily defeated them with his modern weapons and better-trained troops. His conquest wound up changing the whole course of Middle Eastern history and the European understanding of that region. But a British fleet under Admiral Horatio Nelson destroyed the French fleet off the coast of Egypt. Unable to get reinforcements, Napoleon abandoned his army to return to France as a conquering hero in the spring of 1799.

The Directory was losing its legitimacy, and some of its leading members were looking for a way to save the revolution. A group of major politicians set up a plot to put Napoleon in power. His heroic reputation and backing by the army would create a stronger, more popular regime. Two key players were Charles Maurice de Talleyrand-Périgord, a noble former bishop, and the onetime priest Abbé Emmanuel Joseph Sieyès. Both had been important but relatively moderate early revolutionary leaders in 1789. After Thermidor Sieyès had become one of the most powerful members of the government, and Talleyrand was the Directory's foreign minister. Along with Napoleon's brother Lucien Bonaparte and other allies, they engineered a coup on the 18th of Brumaire (month of fog), year VIII (November 9, 1799) that put Napoleon in power as first consul of a new government called the Consulate. Sieyès and others sought to have Napoleon rule with them, but he quickly outmaneuvered them to make himself military dictator.[22]

This coup became an iconic example of how an army could overthrow a revolution, and Bonapartism ever since has been used as a convenient term for the kind of regime established by Napoleon. It turned France into an exceedingly aggressive but far more conservative dictatorship than had originally been envisioned by even the original moderate revolutionaries. It was famously seized upon by Karl Marx to scathingly denounce the 1851–1852 coup by Napoleon's nephew, Louis Napoleon (later Napoleon III), to seize power.[23] But Marx's justifiable hatred of Napoleon III led him astray. He wrongly wrote that Bonapartism lacked a coherent ideological base. Actually the first Napoleon was the reasonable conservatives' solution to the revolution, keeping and extending many of its Enlightenment reforms while shutting down all possibility of radical extremism, democracy, or popular protest. It allowed much of the prerevolutionary elite to regain its property and prestige, but it also let in the new elites that had emerged during the revolution by creating another layer of nobility. It appealed to nationalists by engaging in expansionary imperialism. It even accommodated itself to the Catholic Church while keeping the church under control. Napoleon III would follow the same program when he established France's Second Empire, though France was by then less powerful and had to direct its imperialism overseas. Ultimately the junior Napoleon would also lead France into disaster in 1870.

As Napoleon's power as first consul grew, his socially conservative side emerged more strongly. In 1802 he reinstituted slavery, abolished earlier by the revolution, in France's remaining colonies and promulgated openly racist decrees against blacks. This was part of his exceedingly vicious attempt to retake Haiti where he had sent an army. He betrayed the relatively moderate Haitian leader, Toussaint Louverture, and set off a terrible civil war in Haiti. His plan to use Haiti as the base for a reconstituted French American Empire came to ruin as the freed slaves fought back, and their resistance, combined with disease, wiped out most of the French army. The destruction and divisions thus created in an independent Haiti isolated by the European powers and the United States left a terrible legacy in that country from which, in some ways, it has never recovered.[24]

Later, when the Napoleonic Code was completed in 1807 and became a template for French and much other European law, Napoleon made sure to take back the advances in women's rights that the revolution had promulgated. Women were once again subordinated to their husbands and fathers, and some of these laws were not to be changed in France until after World War II.[25]

Napoleon made himself emperor in 1804, thus ending the First French Republic and creating the First Empire. He went on to conquer most of Europe, but bled his country dry by expending its resources and drafting so many young men. Up to a million died, not counting other casualties. His ever-growing megalomania finally ended in disaster. He invaded Spain, but there the French got bogged down in an interminable guerrilla war. Then he invaded Russia in 1812 to force it to adhere to his continental blockade of England. This resulted in a catastrophic defeat that wiped out his army. He returned to France and raised a new army, but he was so weakened that France was beaten back and invaded by a coalition of European powers. Napoleon was forced to abdicate and go into exile on the small Italian island of Elba in 1814. In 1815 he returned and ruled France for another one hundred days, only to lead its army to another disaster at Waterloo. The British then sent him into permanent exile on the remote island of Saint Helena, where he died of stomach cancer in 1821 at the age of fifty-one.[26]

As the French Revolution had become ever more dependent on its army, it was almost inevitable that a military dictatorship would ensue. The dictator could have been someone other than Napoleon—for example, the equally brilliant but more cautious revolutionary general Jean-Baptiste Bernadotte. If France had gotten less of a megalomaniac as military dictator, it might have sought peace after some of its initial great successes. Instead, it got Napoleon.[27]

The French are still debating his legacy. While the left increasingly recognizes that he was a tyrant who ruined his country, many, particularly conservatives, continue to lionize him as a great Enlightenment liberal who helped modernize all of Europe. Ever the realist, however, the conservative and publicly grandiose Charles de Gaulle, France's greatest twentieth-century hero, believed that Napoleon had badly damaged France.[28]

So, we might ask, why was there no Soviet Napoleon when the Red Army and its generals played such a crucial role in saving the revolution? Given Marx's hostility to Napoleon I's betrayal of the democratic French Revolution, and the close reading of French revolutionary history by Lenin and his top associates, it is not surprising that, once in power and forced to create a large Red Army, they greatly feared the potential rise of Bonapartism. Partly to preclude that and to control the army, they installed Bolshevik political commissars in the army. Every general had such a political co-commander. Stalin was one of them, as were many other top party members.

Was that enough? Trotsky, though himself very close to Lenin and in many ways the number two Bolshevik leader, became the founder and leader of a great Red Army that eventually included five million men. To many of his officers and men, he was a brilliant, charismatic hero without whom the civil wars could not have been won. He was also a great orator and writer. Had he wanted to, could he have become the Russian Revolution's Napoleon, as many top Bolsheviks came to fear he would?

In 1922, before his first stroke that year, Lenin appointed Stalin to be general secretary of the Communist Party, a post that was important but far from all-powerful. Stalin had from the start been a top Bolshevik, for a time editor of the party newspaper *Pravda*. He was a member of the original 1917 leadership group that ran the party with Lenin. This included Trotsky, Grigory Zinoviev, Lev Kamenev, Grigory Sokolnikov, and Andrei Bubnov (all of whom would eventually be expelled from the party and then murdered on Stalin's orders between 1937 and 1940).

A main reason for Stalin's rise to absolute power from 1924 to 1929, after Lenin's death, was his control over the party machinery that allowed him, as general secretary, to make most key administrative appointments. This let him put his followers and close friends in power. When Stalin took over, he had a staff of about six hundred, but there were tens of thousands of Communist officials spread around the vast country. Stalin was an exceptionally able, hardworking leader who placed roughly four thousand capable people in top positions; but he also managed to reassure many in lesser posts who had recently joined the party, or had been selected by local committees, that they would be guaranteed a place. He appeared—contrary to what he later became, and to the stereotypes put out about him by his enemies—a sympathetic listener who remembered names of top associates, cared for them, and won their loyalty. He could also explain Marxism-Leninism more straightforwardly than did his more intellectually sophisticated colleagues, and this further endeared him to younger, less educated new party members.

Stalin was not a cosmopolitan intellectual like Lenin, Trotsky, Kamenev, or Zinoviev, the most important other leaders, and they, especially Trotsky, looked down on him as a mediocre boor who did not know other major European languages as they did, and was not as fluent a writer.[29] How mistaken they were!

Trotsky, for all his brilliance, was openly arrogant and irked many of the other top leaders. He was also a party loyalist who had no wish to act against it, though he assumed that as Lenin's effective second in command he would be recognized as the new leader. But Stalin joined with Kamenev, Zinoviev, and other top leaders to mobilize against Trotsky. The main policy question was whether to continue the NEP, or, as Trotsky wanted, to emphasize instead a theoretically more pure socialism. Trotsky also wanted to continue efforts to spread Marxist-Leninist revolutions elsewhere. At this point, however, most party members were fearful of yet more international complications that might bring new wars, and were in favor of more cautious internal consolidation. This position favored Stalin, and his friend Bukharin justified it in his writing on theoretical grounds.[30]

Stalin (who hated Trotsky—the feeling was mutual) advocated continuing to build party power in the Soviet Union, and not pushing too hard with socialism so as to not alienate peasants and workers. He seemed more reassuring than Trotsky and had thousands of loyal party officials, along with the Central Committee (effectively the Soviet parliament), to back him. Trotsky, who personally abhorred petty plotting, and his supporters were easily marginalized. Eventually he was completely isolated, expelled from the party, and forced into exile. In 1940 he would be murdered in Mexico by an NKVD (secret police) hit man.

Could Trotsky have become a Napoleon, as some Bolsheviks feared? He would have had to seize power when he still commanded the Red Army in 1921 and was at the height of his prestige while Stalin still had no power base. It seems never to have occurred to him; it would, in any case, have been completely contrary to his belief that the party had to be in charge. But Lenin, to whom he was loyal, was its undisputed leader. By the time Lenin died in 1924, Trotsky no longer controlled the army, and it was too late, though even then he thought his prestige and record alone would save him. The fact that Trotsky was Jewish, though personally hostile to all religions, also played a role: among new and less educated party members, traditional Russian anti-Semitism was still strong.[31]

What about one of the top Red generals, particularly the leading proponent of the need to prepare for advanced mechanized warfare with tanks and airpower, Mikhail Tukhachevsky? He had many times proved his military leadership skills and devotion to the party, including when he had led the repression of the Kronstadt revolt in 1921. Stalin had clashed with him earlier during the civil wars but agreed with his understanding of modern warfare and needed his skills. He never trusted him, however, and called him "Napoleonchik" (little Napoleon). In 1931 Tukhachevsky was made deputy commissar for defense responsible for modernizing the Red Army, which he did, but he no longer commanded any troops directly. Nor was he particularly well liked, given his penchant for high living, his many mistresses, and his personal arrogance. Stalin, who had not felt secure enough in 1930 to get rid of this most dangerous, brilliant soldier, had become unquestioned dictator by 1937. He then had Tukhachevsky arrested, tortured, and shot. He also liquidated his immediate family. It was not just Tukhachevsky who worried him, however, but the entire high military command, because by the late 1930s they were the only conceivable source of opposition. So he had most of them murdered in 1937–1938: 3 of 5 marshals, 15 of 16 army commanders, 60 of 67 corps commanders, 136 of 199 divisional commanders, and in all about 40,000 of lesser ranks were killed.[32] By that time, most of the old Bolshevik leaders had also perished. (We will return to this in a later chapter.) But Stalin and his repressive secret police were too unshakably in command for any opposition, military or otherwise, to resist.

So there wasn't any chance for a Napoleon to emerge, and never in the entire history of Communist Party rule in other countries has there ever been a successful military coup, because similar preventative measures were taken in all of them. Some people really do learn from history.

In Russia, from the start of the Bolshevik Revolution, with the liberals and moderate socialists out of power, there was a Communist Party with its structured hierarchy, powerful ideology, and great leaders. Civil war necessitated the building of a large army, but, equally, a very strong repressive apparatus controlled by the party. The more bitter the struggles, mostly within Russia itself, the stronger the Cheka and the ruling party became. In fact, Stalin was the Bolsheviks' Napoleon, but as party head rather than as a military man. He was as much the natural product of the revolutionary conflicts as Napoleon had been. Had it been Trotsky, or some other top Bolshevik, who had come to power instead of Stalin, there would still have been a repressive dictatorship, a push to create socialism no matter what the cost, and a lot of deaths. There probably would not have been as much paranoia and killing, but neither Trotsky nor any of the other top Bolsheviks would have hesitated to apply cruel means to transform Russia. What the outcome might have been had Stalin not been the winner we can never know. The Trotskyites who have always thought that their hero could have made socialism work better have underplayed Trotsky's own brutality, commitment to class warfare, and determination to create an entirely new kind of society; but perhaps his rule would indeed have been somewhat less traumatic.

Using War and Foreign Danger to Purge Enemies:
Hitler, Mao, and Khomeini

In 1933 the Nazis came to power legally in Germany, but to consolidate their dictatorship, they needed visible, immediate foreign enemies. Jews and Communists and by association the entire left were identified as treacherous foes. Conveniently the Reichstag, the German parliament, caught fire and burned down on February 27, 1933, a month after Hitler had come to power. There used to be some controversy as to whether the arson was a Nazi plot meant to provoke the kind of fear that would legitimize a host of repressive measures, or whether it was really committed by a Dutch former Communist found on the premises. The most recent scholarship makes it practically certain it was a Nazi plot, and that they had planted a misled, hapless scapegoat. It worked and allowed the Nazis to steamroller a set of new laws, signed by President Hindenburg, that gave them absolute power and killed democracy. Hindenburg may have despised Hitler, but he and his entourage hated the Communists and the Social Democrats far more.[33] This was neither the first nor the last time in history such a ploy would be used to kill potential opposition to dictatorial repression, but it was certainly one of the most successful.

Hitler never intended to lead a peaceful regime. Not only did the Nazis immediately launch a campaign of violence and terror in Germany; they also began preparing Germany for war right away. Fascism in general was typically aggressively nationalistic, and the movement glorified war. As Benito Mussolini put it in "La dottrino del fascismo" in 1932's *Enciclopedia Italiana*, "War alone brings up to their highest tension all human energies and imposes the stamp of nobility upon the people who have the courage to make it." But after the horrors of World War I, some special justification was needed, and fabricated or exaggerated events that served this end were always useful. It was therefore essential to play up outside threats from communists, combined with nationalist resentment against France's role in imposing the humiliating Versailles Treaty.

To accomplish this, Hitler needed to ensure the loyalty of an army that resented the influence of Brownshirt (SA) thugs but was eager to have itself well funded and restored to its old strength. He also had to show Germany's conservative elites that the more extreme parts of his domestic agenda—specifically any hint of the socialism embedded in the party's name—would not be pushed too hard. This coincided with Hitler's own suspicion that some Nazi radicals might question his leadership. To solve these problems, on June 30, 1934, Hitler launched the Night of the Long Knives. Ernst Röhm, a longtime Hitler friend and ally who commanded a paramilitary force of about two million SA members, was murdered. The SA were neutralized, to be ultimately replaced by Heinrich Himmler's SS. But Hitler used the purge to pass yet more repressive measures, to consolidate his power, and to set Germany on the path to war, which was his main goal.[34] (See below, in chapter 4, for more detail about the SA, the SS, and Hitler's rule.)

Threats, whether from wars, internal divisions, or the pretense that such dangers exist, have repeatedly been deployed by revolutionary leaders to purge those who challenge their power, and to impose ever more repression. It is a strategy that continues to be used by antidemocratic forces everywhere.

There is another analogous if not entirely parallel example. The Chinese Communist Party came to power as the result of over two decades of wars against foreign and domestic enemies. By the time of their final victory in 1949, they had already developed the military and repressive machinery that solidified their control over their party and army, and had developed many of the institutions that they would use to create a strong dictatorship. This did not mean, however, that Mao Zedong had not already engineered purifying purges within the party to consolidate his rule. The pressures of the civil war that eventually led him to victory also legitimized these purges, which is why the quote at the start of this chapter is so apt. And as might have been expected, domestic and foreign threats, both real and fabricated, were used to conduct many further purges after 1949. The cry that the revolution is threatened, so the party must be purged of corruption and traitors, was as frequently used by Mao as it was by Stalin. It continues to be a favorite trope of the

Chinese Communist Party's leadership to this day.[35] (For much more on the Chinese Revolution, see chapter 4 below.)

The story in Iran after 1979 is more obviously similar to that of the French Revolution after 1789 and the Russian one after 1917. We have already seen in the previous chapter how radical clerical rule under Khomeini was not imposed immediately after the overthrow of the shah. Compromises had to be made to accommodate more moderate supporters, and Khomeini was careful to move gradually. What greatly helped him accelerate the realization of his ideological goal—creating a radical Islamic theocracy—was the threat posed by domestic uprisings, by the perceived threat of American intervention, and most of all by a brutal Iraqi invasion of Iran.

In the chaos of the revolution, there were a number of ethnic and regional uprisings by groups trying to seize land, gain more autonomy, and perhaps even foster secession. Kurds (there were about four million, 10 percent of the total Iranian population) who were mostly in the northwest, Turkmen in the northeast, Arabs in the southwest, and Baluchis in the southeast were the main disaffected minorities that had felt repressed by the shah. When there were localized rebellions in their regions in 1979, they were bloodily crushed with bombings, massacres, and many thousands of executions. Though the Kurds fought on for several more years, the regime was never seriously threatened. The repression did, however, bring to the fore a longtime Khomeini ally, Sadegh Khalkhali, who was made chief justice of the Revolutionary Court. He presided over not only the executions in these regions, but also those of thousands of former officials, leftists, and other real and potential enemies of the regime, earning him the nickname of Iran's "hanging judge."[36]

The regime's first prime minister, Mehdi Bazargan, had been a longtime opponent of the shah, but he was also a distinguished university professor and a moderate Muslim. He opposed much of the bloodshed and wanted a reconciliation with the West, including the Americans. What utterly defeated him and gave Khomeini the opportunity to push a more radical agenda was the sudden, unplanned occupation of the American Embassy by radical students on November 4, 1979. Khomeini had not been behind the takeover, but he moved quickly to use it as an excuse to strengthen his hold, claiming that the evidence turned up in the embassy showed that moderates had been colluding with the United States to overthrow the revolution. He reminded Iran that this had happened in 1953 when American intervention had restored the shah. The United States (labeled "the Great Satan") was hardly blameless, given its past record of support for the shah. Bazargan, seeing that he was being outmaneuvered by Khomeini's radicalism, retired on November 6.[37]

Before the seizure of the embassy that resulted in the holding of American diplomats as hostages until January 20, 1981, Khomeini had been consolidating his power, particularly when, three months after coming to power, he set up the equivalent of his own Cheka, the Sepah-e Pasdaran-e Enqelab-e Eslami (Islamic Revolutionary Guard Corps, generally called Sepah, or sometimes the Pasdaran). By September 1979 this corps numbered eleven thousand, who formed the nucleus of what would become the key repressive and military backbone of the regime's radical governing clerics. They soon became active not only within Iran, but also in promoting terrorism and direct military aid in the Middle East to further Iranian power. The seizure of the American Embassy gave them a significant boost.

Repression had begun before the seizure of the American Embassy, but efforts to write a new constitution had been contentious, with significant opposition to giving Khomeini too much power. As the hostage crisis developed, Khomeini was able to use the possibility of American intervention to increase repression and win the referendum that established his preferred version of the constitution in early December 1979. This made Khomeini, and any potential successor as velayat-e faqih (literally guardian jurist), the possessor of supreme power. The guardian jurist was given the right to veto any policy he disliked. Khomeini would hold the position until he died, and his successor, Ali Khamenei, remains in this position for life (as of 2019).

The sudden invasion of Iran by Saddam Hussein's Iraq in September 1979 had an effect similar to the Austrian-Prussian war against France in 1792 and the foreign intervention in Russia in 1918. Patriotic Iranians—

even including much of the country's mostly Shi'a Muslim Arab minority who disliked Iraq's brutal, secular dictatorship, which treated Shi'ites as inferiors—rallied to the regime. Many highly skilled pilots trained by the Americans under the shah had been imprisoned but were now released. Very few defected. Their use of the superior American aircraft, along with their better training, overwhelmed the Russian-equipped and -trained Iraqi air force, and it was Iran's air force that made a major contribution in defeating the first, seemingly overwhelming Iraqi invading forces.

The Iran-Iraq War turned into a hugely damaging, bloody, deadlocked affair that ended only in 1988. At least a quarter of a million Iranians died, and over three hundred thousand were disabled. Some estimates double the number of dead. The Iraqi losses were probably about the same. Iran's economy was devastated. But there was a greater measure of national solidarity, and throughout the war repression continued, with imprisonments and executions. By the end of the war in 1988, the radical religious regime led by Khomeini was very solidly entrenched.[38]

As with the French and Russian revolutionary wars, the Iranian regime's survival under extreme stress facilitated and consolidated the victory of the more radical forces against the relative moderates. Repression and terror intensified even as the external threat increased.

But though in Iran the extremists seemed to have won, the outcome has not been the same as in the Stalinist Soviet Union, but rather closer to what happened in France. After Khomeini died in 1989, there was a partial, gradual Thermidorian reaction. Iran remains dominated by its clerics and is far from being a democracy, but some reformist presidents have been allowed. There are arrests, tortures, and killings of opponents, but also some liberties that not even the post-Stalinist Soviet Union would have tolerated until the late 1980s. Iran intervenes actively in the Middle East and has provided crucial support to Syria's brutal dictatorship, which has killed hundreds of thousands and caused millions to flee. It supports the violent and dangerous Hezbollah party in Lebanon, and stirs up trouble by supporting Shi'ites elsewhere in the region, but it does not want to isolate itself. Its foreign policy is militant, but as in

France after Thermidor, Iran is internally divided between more moderate forces and its radicals. The Revolutionary Guard, now the mainstay of the radical forces, has become increasingly corrupt because of its economic power, so the economy is therefore less efficient, but it is not entirely government controlled. As in the period of the Directory in France from 1794 to 1799, the future of the Iranian Revolution remains uncertain, at least as of the late 2010s.[39]

4

The Tyranny of Idealistic Certitude and Imagined Utopias

It is untrue that I or anybody else in Germany wanted war in 1939. . . .
[T]hose who carry the real guilt for the murderous struggle, this
people will also be held responsible: the Jews! . . . I call upon the
leadership of the nation and those who follow it to observe the racial
laws most carefully, to fight mercilessly against the poisoners of all the
peoples of the world, international Jewry.

—ADOLF HITLER'S LAST TESTAMENT ONE
DAY BEFORE HE COMMITTED SUICIDE[1]

The possibility of dictatorship is implicit in any regime based on a
single, irremovable party. . . . And irremovability was merely another
name for the total conviction of the Bolsheviks that the Revolution
must not be reversed and that its fate was in their hands. . . . Stalin
showed a sound sense of public relations. . . . His terrifying career
makes no sense except as a stubborn, unbroken, pursuit of that utopian
aim of a communist society to whose reassertion he devoted the last of
his publications, a few months before his death.

—ERIC HOBSBAWM[2]

FERVENT REVOLUTIONARY UTOPIANS wanted to transform their
societies no matter how much force had to be used because, after all,

they were so certain their fantasies could—no, *must be* birthed. Once in power, abandoning those ideologies that had enabled them to overcome so many challenges was out of the question.

Alas, the more transformative the utopia, the more likely it was to meet inevitable, practical barriers. No utopia yet devised fully took into account the imperfections of normal human behavior. The most drastic of revolutionary extremists, whether Robespierre's Jacobins, Lenin's Bolsheviks, Mao's or the Khmer Rouge's Communists, Hitler's Nazis, or Khomeini's Islamists, have all run into common problems: greed, corruption, and the unwillingness of most people to voluntarily sacrifice everything for a future, unattainable heaven on earth. Therefore the ideologues' pursuit of drastic transformation inevitably met resistance from those whose well-being, faith, or lives were at risk. So, over time, hundreds of millions paid the price in mass murders, wars, and the economic catastrophes produced by the utopians in power.

How could this be? If such a revolutionary movement can manage to remain in power, unlike the radical French Jacobins whose Reign of Terror lasted less than two years, it can only be because there are enough followers so dedicated to the ideal, so certain that they are right, that they are willing, at almost any cost, to pursue their goal. They can then organize and direct those less dedicated but who obey out of fear, careerism, or sheer opportunism. But leading cadres must retain their faith. If they do not, the extremism and oppression to sustain it will necessarily wane. Hitler, Stalin, Mao, Pol Pot, Khomeini, and their closest followers kept their original ideologies to the end of their lives. Rather than accepting the limitations of their utopian dreams, they increasingly applied violence to reshape not only their societies but human nature itself. They died unrepentant, still certain they had been right.[3]

Not all revolutions turn out that way. The ideological essence of the American Revolution was not to reshape the social structure of the thirteen colonies by upending its existing elites. It was a political, but not an economic, social, or cultural revolution. Its leaders never envisioned dictatorship and terror to achieve their goals. There have been many other such far less bloody, less totally transformative revolutions: the

French ones of 1830 and 1848; the Japanese Meiji "Restoration," which was a genuine social, political, and economic revolution, albeit a gradual one without a dramatic reign of terror, that followed the overthrow of the shogunate (see below in chapter 6); and many though hardly all of the anticolonial revolutions of the twentieth century.

A much more confounding case was the Mexican Revolution of 1910–1920 because it had many of the elements that produced so much violence and repression in the Russian, the Chinese, the Iranian, and even the French Revolution of 1789. Yet the Mexican Revolution never became as radical as these others because it didn't formulate a coherent utopian ideal. We therefore need to look at this seeming exception before returning to the examples of tyrannical certitude, revolutionary regimes willing and able to commit bloody excesses in order to bring about their imagined utopias.

The Mexican Anomaly: The Exception That Proves the Rule?

The Mexican Revolution was the first of the major revolutions in the twentieth century and was similar in some ways to those that we have already discussed. In 1910 there was no oblivious king, but there was such a monarch's equivalent. The onetime liberal leader Porfirio Díaz, who was eighty, had been in power since 1876 and had long since become a conservative autocrat out of touch with the rising level of discontent incited by his dictatorial rule. During the Porfirian era, the Mexican state had been substantially reinforced and centralized. Earlier the Mexican state's reach had been limited by powerful regional bosses, so many of these traditional elites resented their loss of status. In 1908 Díaz promised to hold free elections in 1910, but instead kept power by cheating. A liberal protest movement led chiefly by Francisco Madero, who was himself from an elite, rich northern Mexican family, demanded free elections and a revised constitution that would prohibit reelection. As in other cases, allowing some liberalizing reform would have averted what was to follow, but instead Madero was imprisoned. He then escaped to the United States to organize resistance.

As in Russia at the same time, and in Iran sixty years later, Mexico had by 1910 experienced several decades of rapid modernization and real but very unequal, highly unsettling economic progress. The rise of a new capitalist economy, including greatly increased foreign investment and trade, had upended the previously traditional, overwhelmingly rural society (at least 75 percent of the Mexican population), especially in the most dynamic regions. The opportunity to make profits from agricultural exports with sugarcane, cotton, and henequen (for fiber) had prompted the traditional haciendas to take over peasant and village communal property. They were joined also by a rising class of *rancheros*, or middle-class market-oriented farmers. There were new railroads as well as mining and textile industries, mostly owned by Europeans or Americans, and with them a new working class. In the new industries there were repeated strikes that were violently suppressed. Peasants who were losing the protection they had had under the traditional hacienda system—which dated back to colonial times—were disaffected, but so were parts of the old rural elite and landowning class that felt their political power fading. There arose some nationalist grumbling about foreign ownership of key enterprises, though perhaps not as much as was later portrayed by nationalist and leftist mythology. In 1907 there had been a serious depression triggered by the panic of 1907 in the United States, so that discontent was exacerbated. So there were clear parallels to conditions in 1788 France and 1978 Iran.

The revolution broke out in 1910 as a response to the stolen election. Not surprisingly, it developed first in the advanced regions of the north, near the American border, where the economy had been the most transformed by foreign investment and trade. That was where many key leaders would come from: Francisco Madero, Álvaro Obregón, Venustiano Carranza, Plutarco Elías Calles, and the still very young Lázaro Cárdenas, all of them future Mexican presidents. Pancho Villa, who for a while seemed on the verge of becoming ruler of Mexico, was another northerner, from Durango, but his base was Chihuahua, also on the American border and one of the most economically transformed areas. Another deeply affected region was just south of Mexico City, Morelos, where commercial sugar plantations had taken over much of the land.

It was in Morelos that the most highly romanticized revolutionary hero, Emiliano Zapata—who was from a prosperous peasant family—became leader of a protest movement demanding that land be given to the peasants. The more backward, less economically dynamic southern part of Mexico, however, was mostly passive during the revolution.

It did not take long for Díaz to understand that the game was up, so he resigned to go live in exile in 1911. He died in Paris in 1915. (Why has Paris been so common a place of refuge for political exiles and potential revolutionaries? That is worth a whole book.) Madero, who had run as a presidential candidate in 1910 but had been cheated of victory, became president in 1911.[4]

President Madero was the quintessential liberal revolutionary, aware of neither how much popular resentment had built up against the old regime, nor how dangerous reactionary forces could be. Zapata led a revolt for land reform in Morelos, and Pascual Orozco, joined by Villa, did the same in Chihuahua. Madero relied on General Victoriano Huerta of the regular army to put down the northern rebellion. After that was done, in 1913 Huerta turned against the revolution, had Madero murdered, and made himself president. Using military brutality, he attempted to return to the old regime. Woodrow Wilson, the new American president—who really did believe in liberal democracy, despite his pronounced racism—disliked Huerta and refused to support him. Civil war erupted, with Zapata and Villa taking prominent roles. Villa managed to draw most of Chihuahua, except for the major landowners, to his side and assembled an effective revolutionary army. Venustiano Carranza, a wealthy northern landowner, led another anti-Huerta movement. His army was led by Álvaro Obregón, the outstandingly able revolutionary general, who understood modern warfare and how to use the advanced weapons the American let him obtain. Obregón and Carranza's army allied itself with Villa and Zapata. In 1914 the United States occupied the Caribbean port of Veracruz, and that was the last straw for Huerta, who fled. (He then collaborated with German agents to try to mount an anti-American coup in Mexico, but was imprisoned by the Americans and died in 1916 in El Paso, Texas.) Carranza became the leader and called for a constitutional convention. But Carranza was another moderate who was not eager to carry out a promised land reform, so Villa and Zapata broke with him and occupied Mexico City. In November 1914 the Americans departed from Veracruz, opening that port city to Carranza's forces, who then were able to resupply themselves. Villa himself, it turned out, did little to reform the part of Mexico he controlled, and Zapata, who was only loosely allied with Villa, was much more interested in transforming his own region than in becoming a truly national figure.

Villa, who insisted on using outdated cavalry charges against Obregón's machine guns and artillery, was defeated in some decisive 1915 battles. The United States recognized Carranza as the leader of Mexico, and Villa, who had counted on American support, was outraged. He struck back by attacking a small town over the border in New Mexico, prompting another American invasion. It yielded no great results, as Villa was able to wage a low-level guerrilla resistance, but he was further marginalized and never regained a major role in the revolution. He would eventually retire as a wealthy hacienda owner, only to be assassinated in 1923 through a plot arranged by Plutarco Elías Calles and President Obregón (though it is not clear which one played the leading role). Zapata was also defeated and pushed into a marginalized guerrilla resistance. He was ambushed and killed by government forces in 1919.[5]

The new constitution was completed in 1917, and Carranza became president of a now mostly united Mexico. In 1919 the commander of Carranza's army, Obregón, declared that he would run for president in 1920 to enact more reforms. Carranza wanted to name his own successor, but he was overthrown and probably murdered on Obregón's orders (though there were rumors that, feeling trapped, he committed suicide). Obregón was then elected under the new constitution to a four-year term from 1920 to 1924. Some serious efforts at land reform were made, but not as extensively as would occur later. More importantly, as early as 1914 Obregón had understood the importance of forging an alliance with a militant workers' union movement, the Casa del Obrero Mundial (COM, the House of the Workers of the World). This not only helped provide his army with a significant workers' urban component, but also guided some of his pro-union policies during his time in power. Subsequently Mexico's unions remained powerful, as they still are today.[6]

Could Obregón, the ultimate victor and dominant general of the revolution, have become the Mexican Napoleon? Or was he, instead, just another in the long line of Mexican and Latin American "caudillos," a traditional strongman-dictator? (Though aside from the fact that France was Europe's strongest power, wasn't Napoleon himself a French caudillo?) Obregón's supporters called him "the Napoleon of the West," and his detractors agreed, emphasizing his forcible seizure of power and his increasingly conservative, dictatorial approach. The historian Jean Meyer wrote that Obregón had wanted to play the role of "first consul" (Napoleon's title after his coup d'état on the 18th of Brumaire).[7] After he took over the presidency again in 1928, he was well on his way to becoming even more Napoleonic. Would he have made himself "president for life?" Before he could retake office, however, he was assassinated by a fanatical Catholic, so we will never know.[8]

According to the Constitution of 1917, reelection was forbidden, so after his four-year term Obregón gave up his office in 1924. Against strong opposition he had his more obscure fellow Sonoran (Sonora was the northern province that produced the most effective revolutionary leaders and armies), Plutarco Elías Calles, elected president, though he had to use military force to impose his will. He had chosen Calles because he believed he could control him, and he remained powerful enough to have the constitution changed so he could retake the presidency in 1928. After his murder, however, the less charismatic but politically shrewd Calles kept control.

Calles was more of a reformer and succeeded in strengthening the Mexican state so that it could no longer be challenged by regional bosses or rebellious generals. But Calles was more than just a pragmatist. He had one egregious ideological fixation, his hatred of the Catholic Church. There had been a long-held liberal dislike and suspicion of the church because it had supported conservatives and was blamed for having blocked the spread of the Enlightenment into Mexico. It had been weakened by the revolution, but remained powerful and, in parts of Mexico, popular. In 1926 Calles therefore launched a full-fledged anti-Catholic war to destroy the church's moral and political authority in order to wean the population away from the reactionary superstitions that he believed had impeded progress for so long. Mexican liberals had admired French Jacobin tradition for a century, so Calles had support, but, not surprisingly, his war became the revolution's most unnecessary and extreme ideological campaign. It met exactly the same kind of resistance as had the French Jacobins' efforts to destroy the Catholic Church. In revolutionary France the war against the church had provoked the bloody Vendée War, and in Mexico from 1926 to 1929 the War of the Cristeros.

The deadly consequences of Calles's insistent anticlericalism confirm the rule that radical ideological fixations promote continuing, extreme violence, sometimes well after the crucial revolutionary civil wars have ended. In some parts of Mexico, particularly the center and west, peasants remained faithful Catholics. Calles's anticlerical measures—closing down churches; persecuting, torturing, and killing priests; and trying to strip the church of influence—provoked a last, bloody counterrevolution. Devout Catholics rose up against the government, as had happened in the Vendée in the 1790s. In Mexico, too, there were terrible massacres and abuses on both sides. About one hundred thousand people died, and at least as many fled. Some American Catholics, led by the Knights of Columbus, supported the Cristeros, while the anti-Catholic Ku Klux Klan, then a powerful political force in the United States, supported Calles. Officially the American government took the side of Mexico's government, as the Cristeros were deemed a disruptive force. Equally important was the fact that both the Vatican and most Mexican high church officials were actually opposed to the Cristeros and sought a peaceful compromise. In the end the American ambassador, Dwight Morrow (coincidentally also Charles Lindbergh's father-in-law), helped by Pope Pius XI, brokered an uneasy truce in 1929. The military leader of the Cristeros, General Enrique Gorostieta (who had earlier fought for the antirevolutionary President Huerta), was killed and the war more or less ended. Nevertheless, Calles remained fixated on his anticlericalism and his wish to produce a secular society. Several thousand more former Cristeros were killed, and there was some continuing violence, though at a lesser level. It was only when Calles lost power in 1935 that a new president abandoned the anticlerical policy entirely and brought the whole matter to a close. The Catholic Church never regained the control of education and official morality that it had once had, but it gradually came to be more tolerated, and Mexico remains an overwhelmingly Catholic country.[9]

Calles did solidify state control, stabilize the currency and economy, and at least supported giving land to peasant communes (the *ejidos*), though not much was done until later. After Obregón's assassination in 1928, Calles kept control and, as "el Jefe Máximo" (supreme leader) of the revolution, appointed presidents who were his puppets until 1934. Here again, the revolution seemed to be turning into a kind of Napoleonic—that is, military—dictatorship that was far more conservative than what the radical revolutionaries had wanted, but the regime was also intent on consolidating the rationalizing, state-building aspects of the Mexican Revolution. To effect this, Calles created a ruling party, the PNR (National Revolutionary Party), in 1929. That would later become the PRM (Party of the Mexican Revolution), and in 1946 it took on its definitive name, the rather contradictory PRI (Revolutionary Institutional Party), by which time it had become far more "institutional" than "revolutionary."[10] But the Napoleonic option, if it ever had a chance after Obregón's murder, was forestalled by Calles's next decision to appoint another puppet president.

In 1934 Calles installed his ally, former general Lázaro Cárdenas, as president. Cárdenas, however, outmaneuvered Calles and had him exiled in 1935. As president, under a new constitutional arrangement, Cárdenas ruled for six years. He pushed major land reform, nationalized the oil fields in 1938, and benefited from the fact that the American president was Franklin Delano Roosevelt, who was not inclined to try to use force to reverse this move, despite some pressure to do so. It was Cárdenas who ended the official anticlericalism that Calles had pursued and made a full peace with the church. Napoleon had done this too, ending the last remnants of the Vendée uprising and reconciling with the Catholic Church. But Cárdenas was no Napoleon. In 1940 when his term was over, he left office quietly. He was the last of the former revolutionary generals who could have made himself president for life; instead, more closely resembling George Washington, he chose to follow the constitution, thus setting the pattern of six-year-long single terms that the PRI honored until it eventually lost power in 2000. Mexico still adheres to the six-year rule. What was left, however, was not exactly a democracy. Rather, it was single-party rule that created a myth of its continuing revolutionary agenda while in a sense betraying Cárdenas's legacy by becoming much more conservative. Never again would the PRI be led by as committed a reformer as Cárdenas had been during his 1934–1940 term in office. His successors who would win unfair, rigged elections did, nevertheless, allow some opposition, even as the PRI and the institutions it had set up became increasingly corrupt because there was no serious check on their power.[11]

So what conclusion can we draw? There is no neat narrative that can encompass all of this chaotic fighting; the betrayals; the mixed, shifting alliances of various regions, interests, and classes that backed one or another of the revolutionary generals; and the final victory of the northern generals. One of the revolution's most famous leaders, Pancho Villa, shifted his ideology often, and it has remained impossible to say exactly what would have happened had he won and become president instead of being essentially limited to his power base in Chihuahua. Emiliano Zapata had a far clearer egalitarian ideology but never moved far from his own base in Morelos.[12] The other major leaders held inconsistent goals. Even the final victors were not ideologically uniform. During the revolution there was no single party. That came only later, in 1929, and though it would monopolize power for the next seven decades, what would eventually be called the PRI was never totalitarian. A unifying ideology only gradually came together, and it wasn't very radical.

That the outcome was not as radical as some subsequent major revolutions of the twentieth century does not mean that the Mexican Revolution avoided catastrophic tragedy. What could have been a moderately reformist regime under Madero turned into an unanticipated, terribly violent, bloody, and extremely destructive civil war. During the main fighting period, from 1911 to 1920, at least five hundred thousand were killed, and a roughly equal number died from disease and famine caused by the fighting, not counting the casualties in the 1926–1929 war of the Cristeros. There were terrible massacres, tens of thousands of executions, and hundreds of thousands fled to the United States or were otherwise displaced, out of a total population of just over fifteen million. This was proportionately almost as bad as the Russian Revolution's civil wars. By 1920, despite its high birthrate, Mexico had fewer people than in 1910. But because there was no coherent radical ideology, there was repression and killing but never anything as sinister or all-powerful as Lenin and Stalin's Cheka, OGPU, NKVD, or KGB. The tragedy, at least as far as widespread killing went, ended after 1929.

All this has led many historians and critics to question whether the Mexican was a revolution at all. Yet the revolution gave labor unions and peasants real influence, and it created a new bureaucratic-political elite, in effect a new Mexican social structure and political system.[13] Nor should we neglect the changes in Mexico's culture. The revolution mythologized and celebrated the pre-Columbian Mexican past that has since become an ingrained part of Mexico's identity. The politically radical Mexican school of painters, most famously Diego Rivera, Frida Kahlo, and José Orozco (but many others too), became the most visible, but hardly the only artistic and literary manifestations of this major cultural transformation.[14]

There was no united radical ideology in the 1910s or early 1920s, something possessed by Communists and the Nazis when they came to power. Nor was there a single charismatic leader who survived in power. The last generals to rule did not try to create a totalitarian state with a killing machine after the fighting was done. Calles's anticlericalism was the only approximation of such a development, and it ended when the Cristeros were defeated and Calles was ultimately exiled. As a result, the catastrophic excesses that have characterized the most extreme modern revolutions, once they were in power, did not occur. Rather, the contradictory ideological elements at play and the conflicting personalities in some ways resembled what had happened in France from 1794 to 1799 after the Thermidorian reaction against the Terror, except that there was no Napoleon to take over, only an eventual slide into moderation and corruption.

How Could Nazism's Ideological
Nightmare Succeed So Well?

When the Nazis came to power on January 30, 1933, they already had a
revolutionary program in mind. They would eliminate Jews from Germany and destroy the Social Democratic and Communist parties. The
democratic Weimar Republic was to be replaced by a Nazi dictatorship
led by Adolf Hitler. Germany would rearm and eventually move not
only to reclaim what it had lost in World War I, but also to extend its
territory to the east in order to gain needed agricultural land and vital
resources for its people. The German "Aryan" race was to be purified,
with the eradication of those who were unfit and non-Aryan—not just
Jews but the disabled, homosexuals, Roma, and other "undesirables."
All this was well known, at least by those who had bothered to read
Hitler's autobiography and program for the future, *Mein Kampf*, published in 1925. There he had written:[15]

> Blood mixture and the resultant drop in the racial level is the sole
> cause of the dying out of old cultures; for men do not perish as a re-
> sult of lost wars, but by the loss of that force of resistance which is
> contained only in pure blood. All who are not of good race in this
> world are chaff.

And:

> For Germany . . . the only possibility for carrying out a healthy ter-
> ritorial policy lay in the acquisition of new land in Europe itself . . . it
> could be obtained by and large only at the expense of Russia.

And also:

> If we pass all the causes of the German collapse [at the end of World
> War I] in review, the ultimate and most decisive remains the failure
> to recognize the racial problem and especially the Jewish menace.

It was all there before 1933, including the history of rising street violence,
murder, and the mobilization of a growing paramilitary Brownshirt SA
(Sturmabteilung, or Storm Detachment) thugs.

Once the party was in power, laws were passed to carry out the Nazi program. The Nazi Party had built up a whole organization led by cadres dedicated to its principles and almost entirely loyal to Hitler. This made the takeover of the German state relatively easy, especially as most of the bureaucracy and military fell in line. Those Nazis deemed less loyal were purged in 1934 in the Night of the Long Knives (see above toward the end of chapter 3 and that chapter's note 34.) When the SA was neutralized in 1934, it was replaced by the even more sinister SS (Schutzstaffel, or Protection Squadron), led by Heinrich Himmler. The SS would grow from a small institution of Hitler's guards to a giant, all-powerful organization, including special elite fighting divisions, as managers of the concentration camps, and as enforcers throughout conquered Europe from 1939 to 1945.[16]

Unlike the Bolsheviks, however, the Nazis never had to fight a civil war to take power. The street violence they fostered killed people, but it can hardly be classified as the kind of conflict that had convulsed revolutionary Russia or, for that matter, Mexico. Nazi violence was at first directed internally against Jews, Communists, and other "impure" racial elements and opponents, but it was on a far vaster international scale that Germany's full military might was deployed from 1939 to 1945.[17]

That there was no dramatic German civil war when the Nazis took power does not mean there was no revolution. German society was drastically changed. The kind of repressive totalitarian politics that emerged under Nazi rule had never before existed except that something similar had begun a few years earlier in the Soviet Union. Even Mussolini's original fascist dictatorship was much less thorough and violent, at least within Italy, if not in its African colonies where it engaged in genocidal wars. In Nazi Germany a new party elite became the ultimate source of power. The economy was not nationalized, but the government began a highly stimulative policy that ended the Depression. Over time, as the economy shifted to a war footing, central government planning organized by Hermann Göring's "Four-Year Plan" took over important sectors more directly. Göring also created the feared Gestapo (Geheime Staatspolizei—secret state police) before turning it over to Himmler's SS. The Gestapo would terrorize all of occupied

Europe during the war. Independent social groups, what is conventionally called "civil society," were shut down or stripped of their functions and replaced by a whole set of cultural, sports, social, labor, and youth organizations dedicated to the construction of a new *Volksgemeinschaft* (a solidary community of the nation's people) that was supposed to overcome the alienation of modern life while molding the people, especially the youth, into loyal, militant Nazis. Not all of this worked as anticipated, of course, but it did break down many traditional social bonds and start to raise a new generation of Hitler youth. The goal was to "coordinate" (*Gleichschaltung*) all aspects of society into a harmonious, totally obedient Nazi mold. Any resistance was ruthlessly crushed.

German conservatives who did not necessarily approve of Nazism's most extreme promises nevertheless believed that Hitler could be controlled, that he and his party would never deliver on their most outrageous promises, and that in the meantime Nazi rule would curb the left and make Germany great again. There was some passive resistance, but as the regime became stronger, by the late 1930s, its efforts at reshaping the society became ever more radical, so whatever feeble resistance there had originally been offered became even weaker. Had Germany won the war, a dramatically new society would have emerged. That Nazism failed had more to do with the short time it had to remake Germany in its own image and with the disruption brought by the catastrophic war, rather than with a lack of revolutionary intent or because Germans resisted.[18]

The rise of fascism after World War I fed on decades of prior intellectual dissatisfaction with supposedly boring and corrupt bourgeois democracy. World War I's carnage immensely strengthened skepticism about the virtues of the liberal Enlightenment. The material and human disaster of the war created mass discontent, and the Depression that began in 1929–1930 made it all much worse. Extreme nationalism had contributed to the world war, but for those who were not attracted to the socialist or communist solutions to social and economic problems, fascism provided a welcome ideology promising relief and reaffirmation of an honorable identity. Hitler, like Mussolini before him, and other right-wing extremist leaders throughout Europe capitalized on all this and had the backing of substantial portions of both elites and the masses. Fear of the left played a major role, though that was exacerbated by fabricated conspiracy theories blaming easily identified targets: Jews, communists, foreigners, bankers, or even what Mussolini called "pluto-cratic" domineering nations, namely, France and the United Kingdom. The success of such fascist ideologies in Germany and Italy was an in-spiration throughout the world, from Japan to Argentina, and as a re-sponse to Anglo-French colonialism in the Middle East.[19]

There is no better confirming case than the rise and fall of Nazism to show that a strong revolutionary utopian ideology held as an absolute faith, if its believers come to power, will lead to immense human tragedy. Not only that, but the catastrophe will continue and even worsen for years after the revolutionaries' conquest of power. For those who be-lieved, Nazism was going to create an idyllic world for Germans, but for conquered inferior "chaff" it promised hell on earth or death.

The consequences are well known. Overall in Europe about forty million died as a result of German aggression and the ensuing war. Most grievously hurt was the Soviet Union, where half or more of those deaths occurred. Of the roughly ten million Soviet military deaths, about three million were Soviet prisoners of war who died of starvation, exposure to the cold, disease, and murder in German prisoner-of-war camps. There were at least another ten million civilian deaths in the parts of the Soviet Union occupied by Germany. These were within what Timothy Snyder has called the "bloodlands" of Central and East-ern Europe. At least five million Jews were among the dead in these bloodlands; the majority were Polish, and two million or more came from other occupied parts of this area, including the Baltic republics and what are now Belarus and Ukraine, but were then in the Soviet Union. This does not include the hundreds of thousands of Jews who perished elsewhere in Europe. British, American, and other Allied armies and civilians accounted for over a million more dead. At least a million were killed in the German and Italian occupation of Yugosla-via and the accompanying civil war. Nor did Germany escape the con-sequences: it suffered just over five million military deaths, about half of which were in the last year of the war. That does not count all the injuries. Allied bombing of Germany was the main cause of civilian deaths, and again close to half were in the last year of the war. Then there were the added deaths among Germany's allies.[20] The human costs of the twelve-year Nazi period were gigantic, and by the end much of Europe lay in ruins.

Nazi ideology and Hitler's obsession with supposed Aryan superiority not only led to aggression and genocide, but also doomed Germany's goal of domination. It is well known that by so badly treating Slavic populations in the Soviet Union, the Germans deprived themselves of support that could have greatly helped them in their war effort, and instead provoked anti-German partisan warfare. The most obvious example was the terrible treatment of Ukrainians, many of whom had naively believed that the Germans would free them from Stalinist oppression.[21]

Equally foolish, though not as genocidally brutal, was Hitler's treatment of France. In *Mein Kampf* he had singled out France as Germany's eternal enemy. After France was defeated in 1940 and a collaborationist regime had been established in Vichy, the authoritarian, anti-Semitic "French State" did all it could to persuade the Germans that it was willing to help as a loyal but autonomous ally. France still had a major fleet, control of its African colonial empire, and very important industrial facilities. It passed anti-Semitic laws, and the French bureaucracy and police cooperated with the Germans. Hitler undertook a few symbolic face-saving policies to keep the Vichy government thinking it could get more, but in fact he never meant to treat France as the ally it could have become. As the war became more desperate for Germany in 1942, France was squeezed ever harder and increasingly terrorized, so that what had once been popular support for Vichy evaporated, and more French belatedly began to fight against the occupation. Here as elsewhere, Nazism's ideology made eventual defeat more likely, though of course, had such ideas not lain at the heart of Nazism, it is unlikely that Germany would have tried to rule all of Europe.[22]

Once trapped into the Nazi system of rule headed by leaders whose absolute certitude about the rightness of their cause never flagged, Germany continued to fight to the last. No matter how battered or disenchanted the population became in the face of constant, widespread Allied bombings, defeats, and increasing privations, the ever more repressive governing party and state institutions retained control. The regime lasted until Soviet troops were a couple of blocks away from Hitler's bunker in Berlin and he committed suicide on April 30, 1945. Even then, Hitler's successor, Grand Admiral Karl Dönitz, held out for another week, hoping to negotiate a surrender that would allow some aspects of the Third Reich to survive.

Shortly after the war ended, surveys indicated that about half of the German population still thought that Nazism had been a good idea, but that unfortunately it had ultimately been badly carried out. All the more so was this the case with Germany's generals, who had wanted to surrender with their "honor" intact, as if it had not been irreparably damaged by their loyalty to Hitler's ideology and full knowledge (later almost always denied) of his regime's crimes. Their excuse was that they were fighting to save European civilization from "Asiatic" Bolshevism, and they were vainly hoping that the Americans and British would recognize this and join them in a continuation of the war against the Soviets. These "honorable saviors of European civilization" thought of themselves as patriotic nationalists and simply ignored the mass murder of Jewish and many more millions of other civilians, the terror they had imposed on Europe, and the destruction they had wrought in the name of Nazi ideology.[23]

A Communist Bloodbath: Mature Stalinism's Ideology

After all the deaths and turmoil of the revolutionary period, by the late 1920s Communist rule in the Soviet Union had stabilized, the economy under New Economic Policy (NEP) had rebounded, and Stalin had won the leadership struggle to emerge as Lenin's undisputed successor. Still, this was insufficient for the true believers. The Soviet Union was very far from being a real socialist, advanced society. Even on Marxist theoretical grounds there was reason to doubt that matters had been settled for good, particularly because the NEP had shown that there remained the potential for the revival of an entrepreneurial middle class, and the independent peasantry still made up the majority of the population. Anyway, the NEP was never supposed to be permanent. Disagreement within the party was only about how long it should be allowed.

Karl Marx's theories about the necessity, even the inevitability, of class warfare is evident in most of his writing.[24] That is even more the case with the Leninist version of Marxism. Lenin's intolerance of opposing points of view, and his willingness to use the utmost amount of violence necessary to obtain and stay in power, has already been discussed above. To survive and triumph, the Bolsheviks had created instruments of repressive control: the Cheka, related political police forces, and a large Red Army. These were now available to power the next stage, which would resume the class struggle and move the Soviet Union closer to its socialist ideal, while also strengthening it to resist what Marxist-Leninist theory predicted as almost inevitable, an eventual assault by the capitalist world afraid of the growing appeal of communism.

Even if Stalin had not won the contest for power between 1924 and 1928, the crisis that would have ensued once the Communist Party reaffirmed its ideological roots would have been violent.

If a working-class majority was supposed to provide the essential base for socialism, it was necessary to rapidly enlarge it by industrialization. For this to be done quickly, heavy industry and capital goods had to be privileged, not consumer products. To strengthen the Soviet Union's defensive capacities, military hardware also had to be produced. How to accomplish such a transformation in what was still a backward, mostly rural society of small peasant owners (there were no longer any large estates) was the essential problem. How could agriculture itself be modernized while enough was extracted to feed the growing industrial cities? Producing farming machinery (symbolized by the glorified tractor) would further delay the making of consumer goods. To add to the quandary, industrialization required purchasing some of the advanced technologies available only from the Western capitalist states, and the only way to pay for that was through the export of raw materials and agricultural products. The traditional peasantry, socially and culturally relatively conservative, had benefited from earlier land reforms and also from the revival of free markets during the NEP. So how could peasants be induced, or if necessary forced, to turn over more produce without getting any meaningful payment in return? For years, even under the best estimates, there would be nothing for them to purchase with whatever they were paid.

The solution was going to be a return to the failed policy of the early days of the revolution, collectivization. But now the Communist Party was in firm enough control to enforce its will. Stalin and his allies believed that only in easily supervised, larger units would it be possible to apply modern technology while also extracting more of a surplus to use for industrialization. Collectivization would also eliminate what many in the party had always considered a danger, that leaving peasants alone and continuing the NEP would reintroduce capitalism and undermine the revolution. Along with collectivization there would also be an expansion of large "state farms" that were bigger units run as direct state enterprises with employees rather than peasants herded together into collectives. Young, newer party members wanted to realize socialism's promise, and they approved of what Stalin's winning political coalition decided in 1928–1929. Collectivization was not just Stalin's idiosyncratic idea, but the realization of an ideology that was deemed necessary. Short-term pain was necessary for longer-term socialist success and building a stronger, better Soviet Union.[25]

Collectivization was a disaster. Peasants slaughtered their animals rather than having them confiscated by the collectives. Production went down and peasant resistance flared up. Nikolai Bukharin, who had tried to counter Stalin's policy, had predicted such an outcome and had proposed that the party move more gradually in order to avert dogged resistance. But by the time Stalin's policies had taken effect, Bukharin had been completely marginalized. Stalin was fully committed to the new policy both on ideological grounds and as a matter of practical politics. To admit that he had been wrong would have threatened him, amounting to an admission that socialism was not going to be realized until much later.

To overcome resistance, the party mobilized tens of thousands, mostly urban workers committed to the future of socialism, the secret police, and the army, to go into villages in order to procure large quotas of produce, leaving too little to feed peasants. This was presented to the party loyalists as a necessary war against rich peasants, the kulaks, whose very presence as an exploitative capitalist class would destroy the revolution if they were allowed to survive. Lenin's fantasy about the existence of such a class sparked the hope that class conflict within the peasantry might create supporters of collectivization. But so little was left to feed the villages—especially in the richest soils of Ukraine and in Kazakhstan, where new territories were supposed to be turned to grain production—that the result was mass famine.[26] (See also notes 10 and 19 to chapter 3 and the accompanying text.)

Ultimately between 1931 and 1933, Steven Kotkin suggests, five to seven million died and ten million came close to starving, an unknown number of whom died later owing to the hardships they had undergone. Other estimates range from around eight million deaths to a high of fourteen million, including the many peasants who were deported to labor camps where more died of hunger, disease, and brutal conditions. At the height of the famine Stalin deliberately prevented relief food from going to the most affected areas, and anyone giving food to rural refugees who fled to better-fed towns could be shot. There are pictures of corpses lying on the streets of towns in Ukraine where the campaign took on genocidal proportions. Bodies would get picked up to be buried; some were not yet quite dead but were interred anyway. It was such a horror that by 1934 doubts began to assail even many party loyalists whose faith in the promise of a better future had provided the personnel to enforce this drastic policy. That threatened Stalin directly and set off the next wave of the spreading nightmare.[27]

There had already been show trials of "saboteurs" blamed for shortcomings in economic performance. It is perfectly understandable that for those who strongly believe in a revolutionary ideology, failures cannot be attributed to that ideology's faulty reasoning. Mistakes and particularly long-lasting problems must then be blamed on ideological laxness or, worse, on sabotage by ideological enemies, by treachery, or through the infiltration of spies by foreign powers. There can be little doubt that Stalin believed that such activities were responsible for much that was going wrong, even if he surely must have known that he was casting the net far beyond those actually responsible. Better to catch all the potential class enemies, Trotskyite plotters, and foreign agents by going too far than to let some get away with sabotage by being too picky about legal niceties. Thus, while Stalin could be flexible up to a point about some economic policies, "he normally attributed such failures of policy to poor organization by his subordinates and to the machinations of class enemies. He responded to crisis by administrative reorganization and repressive measures."[28]

Robespierre and Lenin or, for that matter, Trotsky would have completely agreed, and Trotsky himself later wrote that the kulaks had to be eliminated.[29] But in 1934 the immense human tragedy of collectivization took a different turn, becoming a cataclysm that could be, and has been, attributed to Stalin's personality rather than to revolutionary necessity.

Because there was growing concern within the party about Stalin's leadership, even at the level of the Central Committee (the equivalent of a parliament), Stalin unleashed the beginnings of what would within two years turn into a massive, deadly purge that reached its frenzied climax between 1936 and 1938.

It began on December 1, 1934, with the murder of Sergei Mironovich Kirov, one of the early Bolsheviks who was party boss of Leningrad (St. Petersburg's new name after Lenin's death) and one of the top Politburo members. He had approved the forced industrialization campaign and collectivization, but was coming to be viewed as more reasonable, less dictatorial, and more approachable than Stalin. Stalin understood that this was a threat to his hold on power. Did he therefore order Kirov's murder? When it happened, Stalin immediately took charge of the inquiry and made sure that Kirov's death would be attributed to the complicity of his now-powerless old Bolshevik rivals Kamenev and Zinoviev, who were arrested within weeks of the murder. The usual scapegoats, Trotskyites, antiparty plotters, class enemies, and saboteurs, were also implicated. Kirov was within days turned into a posthumous great Soviet hero. Whether Stalin ordered the actual murder remains controversial. There are strong reasons to think he did, but there are reputable scholars who disagree, and there is no documentary proof to confirm his guilt. In any case, almost immediately, within a few days, Stalin used Kirov's murder to begin a purge of supposedly guilty party members. The rapidity with which a vast plot of thousands was conjured up makes it unlikely that this had not been prepared in advance.[30] Stalin, however, wanted more than arrests. He felt it necessary to carefully prepare show trials that would prove to the world the depth of treacherous duplicity that had existed within the ranks of the party. That took more time.

The first top old Bolsheviks to be put on public trial were Kamenev and Zinoviev, whose trial took place in August 1936, a year and a half after their arrests. The "Trotskyite-Zinoviev Center" with Zinoviev and Kamenev as its leaders was exposed as part of a monstrous plot, and the sixteen accused were promptly shot after a completely dishonest show trial. But Stalin had in mind much more, the complete elimination of all possible opposition. In 1937 this expanded into an immense, deadly purge that implicated not only most of the old Bolshevik leaders who had not become Stalin's most trusted, subservient acolytes, but thousands, then millions of other potential class enemies, saboteurs, invented spies, traitors, and in many cases whole families of the accused. According to NKVD files, from 1934 to 1936, including the period when the first wave of arrests over the Kirov murder occurred, 529,434 were arrested, of whom 290,479 were guilty of "counterrevolutionary crimes." But only 4,402 were executed (though how many later died in forced labor camps, the "Gulag," is not counted). In 1937–1938, there were 1,575,259 arrests, 87 percent of which were for political crimes. No exact number of executions is recorded, but, including those who died while being interrogated and tortured, or died on the way to and in camps, the probable number of deaths in those years was about 830,000. There were even quotas by region set up on Stalin's orders. To fulfill them many were randomly arrested.[31]

In 1937–1938 there was a wholescale purging of the military, the only institution that might conceivably have thwarted Stalin, though in fact there never was a plot against him. The majority of top officers were arrested. Most were executed. (See note 32 to chapter 3 and the accompanying text.) Then Stalin went after minority ethnic communities living near the borders, as he believed they were disloyal. The most affected were Poles in the western Soviet Union, hundreds of thousands of whom were deported to camps, with many dying. Ethnic Koreans near the Manchurian border (under the ludicrous and completely misinformed notion that somehow Koreans were allies of the Japanese, who had in fact brutally invaded and colonized their country), Black Sea Greeks, and others were also targeted. Though these and other ethnic groups who were later deported during World War II were not slated for immediate executions, many did die of hardship. For example, something close to half among the Koreans died during transportation, and then of privation after landing in remote parts of Kazakhstan and Uzbekistan.[32] Stalin's paranoia had no limits, and many of those involved in the repression were themselves subsequently liquidated, as were some of those who had been his close associates, even friends.

At the Twentieth Soviet Communist Party Congress in 1956, Nikita Sergeyevich Khrushchev, himself one of the closest of Stalin's henchmen, blamed Stalin for having distorted Lenin's legacy by fostering a cult of personality that had deified him and permitted his cruel and misguided crimes. That made it seem that the party as a whole, and the ideology behind it, were not at fault, only Stalin and a few of his minions.[33] But was this the case? Was it just Stalin's personality, or was there something deeper about the guiding communist ideology that not only made this possible, but made something like it even probable? There are many comparative cases that suggest that if Stalin was excessively paranoid, there were other communist dictators who were at least as much so. China's Mao Zedong, North Korea's Kim Il-Sung and his heirs, Cambodia's Pol Pot, and Albania's Enver Hoxha all persecuted, purged, and killed potential or real class enemies in large numbers, including many in their own revolutionary parties. They executed even former very close associates, and in some cases committed genocidal minority ethnic cleansings. Even relatively less murderous (and only relatively so!) communist dictators like Yugoslavia's Tito and Cuba's Fidel Castro executed and imprisoned many tens of thousands. This also happened in Vietnam under Ho Chi Minh and his successors, who may seem benign compared to their horrific Khmer Rouge neighbors in Cambodia. But they also killed tens of thousands and imprisoned hundreds of thousands. Perhaps a Soviet Union under Trotsky, Zinoviev, or Bukharin would have killed fewer than Stalin, but there can be little doubt based on their record when they did have power, and on their strong ideological commitment, that vast numbers would have died anyway.

There is a psychological element that is related to, but goes beyond, ideology. Power struggles in revolutionary situations not only induce paranoia, but even favor those who are inordinately suspicious in the first place, especially if they come to see their reach for power as necessary to bring about radical, ideologically motivated change. Of course they have enemies, both within their movement and outside it. And those who are not willing to be brutal lose out in chaotic revolutionary situations of unconstrained conflict. Stalin was more than willing.

China's Calamitous Twentieth-Century Revolutions

The Chinese Revolution began in 1911 in a failing empire that was being parceled out bit by bit to European powers and Japan. It overthrew the weak Qing dynasty in 1912. There was a liberal democratic leader, Sun Yat-sen, but it was a more conservative general, Yuan Shikai, who became the first president and then tried to restore the empire until he died in 1916. Then China fell apart into warring regions headed by local warlords. Gradually Sun began to reunify China. On May 4, 1919, nationalist students demonstrated to demand reform and called on China to take back concessions along the coast seized by the major world powers. The demonstration began what came to be called the May 4 Enlightenment Movement, spearheaded by idealistic young intellectuals.

In 1920 Lenin sent Comintern agents to help the growing leftist movement in China. Founded in 1919 and headed by Grigory Zinoviev (later executed by Stalin), the Communist International was tasked with fostering communism beyond Russia. China was fertile ground as Marxist ideas were spreading among intellectuals. In 1921 the Chinese Communist Party (CCP) was founded at a meeting held, ironically, in the protected French territorial concession in Shanghai. Soviet agents, however, also saw Sun's Nationalist Party, the Kuomintang (KMT), as promising and helped turn it into a more disciplined party organized along Leninist lines. (In the pinyin transcription system used in the People's Republic of China, it is Guomindang, whereas Taiwan still uses the old transcription system.) Between 1921 and 1927 the KMT and the CCP were allies. In 1923 Sun sent his young military leader, Chiang Kai-shek (Jiang Jieshi in pinyin) to Moscow to study, and it was Chiang who became the effective leader of the KMT after Sun died in 1925.

Chiang was never much of a believer in democracy and later would shift from being oriented toward Leninism to taking German fascism as his model. In 1927 he broke with the CCP and savagely repressed it, coming close to wiping it out in cities and forcing it into rural retreats where it survived by building a peasant base. As Chiang relied on local elites, land reform was not part of his program. The Communists did push land reform in areas they controlled, and this helped them win converts. Communism's emphasis on reform also appealed to many young urban intellectuals who, over time, would join the movement and provide important support.

By 1928 Chiang had substantially reunited China under Nationalist rule. He was a committed nationalist modernizer, and an effective military leader whose intent was to recover China's lost grandeur. He was personally honest, though the KMT and many of its local allies weren't. He was not, however, strong enough either to force the mostly British, French, and Japanese coastal enclaves out of China, to completely wipe out the Communists, or to bring all warlords under control, particularly in Manchuria.

Because of its resources and location astride the Russian Trans-Siberian Railway to the Pacific Coast, Manchuria was the site of territorial disputes among the local warlord, the Chinese government, the Soviet Unions, and Japan. There was some fighting between Soviet and Japanese forces along the Manchurian-Soviet border, but in 1931 Japan directly occupied all of that province, turning it into the puppet state of Manchukuo, an economically important Japanese colony.

Chiang kept control of most of the rest of the country. In 1934 a desperate Communist Party holding out in rural southeast China was surrounded by KMT forces and had to flee its rural enclaves. In a circuitous route that took a year, it managed to reach the remote northern province of Shaanxi. This "Long March" of over five thousand miles was deadly: most of those who started it lost their lives because of the very poor, harsh terrain they went through and the harassing KMT attacks. This was when Mao Zedong—whose wife was severely injured and who had to abandon one of their children—and his closest assistant, Zhou Enlai, consolidated their leadership positions in the CCP. It was hardly a smooth process, as power struggles within the party were severe and Soviet agents did not support Mao. Furthermore, Stalin continued to see Chiang as a potential ally against Japanese imperialism and was less than fully supportive of the Communists. There were intraparty purges, desertions, and untold numbers of personal tragedies that forged a very harsh but ideologically very committed group of military and political leaders around Mao.

Despite being relatively secure in Shaanxi after their arrival there, the Communists almost certainly would not have emerged as the ultimate victors for control of China had it not been for the 1937 Japanese invasion of highly populated eastern China. Chiang and his Nationalist government were pushed back into more remote areas. In the ugly war from 1937 to 1945, about fifteen million Chinese died, about one-third of whom were civilians massacred by the Japanese. It was the KMT armies that suffered the most casualties, though subsequent mythologizing by the CCP made it seem that Communists had been the main fighters against Japan.

At the sudden end of World War II in 1945, with the Japanese still holding much of China, the Nationalist army was depleted; moreover, it had long relied too much on poorly paid, unmotivated recruits brutally forced into unwilling service. The KMT had also been deeply corrupted by having had to compromise with local elites, and it was too dependent on those to commit to land reform. The Communists, on the other hand, were able to raise a large, mostly peasant People's Liberation Army, and they treated their soldiers much better, inculcating superior discipline and morale. The two sides fought a bitter civil war from 1946 to 1949. The Communists had used the war to build up their resources, and, with the help of a now-allied Soviet Union, they received supplies that helped them defeat Chiang's Nationalists in a large-scale conventional war. The decisive battles were fought in Manchuria, where Chiang's forces were overwhelmed. His main armies defeated, Chiang Kai-shek lost the rest of mainland China, and his remnant KMT forces fled to Taiwan where Chiang massacred tens of thousands of Taiwanese to crush opposition to KMT rule. Ultimately, however, he enacted land reform and led Taiwan's very successful modernization until he died in 1975. All the rest of China became the Communist People's Republic of China (PRC).[34]

The KMT had not been remotely democratic or liberal. If we take into account civilians they massacred for political reasons, military re-cruits who were mistreated and died as a result, and famines caused by KMT depredations and neglect, something on the order of 2.5 to 3 mil-lion people died for noncombat reasons. Probably more than a million of the Nationalist armies' war deaths were due more to the way soldiers were treated by their leaders than to direct warfare. Then, during the last part of the Civil War, until 1949, both sides suffered another 5 million deaths.[35] But this was only the start, as the ideologically disciplined and committed Communist Party was about to launch a series of radical reforms that over the next twenty-seven years would kill even more.

China needed a land reform. Even in areas where there were no lon-ger big landowners, peasant property was unevenly held. But Mao and his Communist Party believed, as did the Russian Communists, that class struggle was necessary to mobilize support and wipe out actual as well as potential class enemies, so the reform was violent. If there were not enough rich peasants in a village, some had to be conjured up. Those designated as class enemies were humiliated, beaten, and—depending on how they were labeled, as either partly guilty "semi-poor" or "aver-age" peasants, or as "rich" ones—executed. Two to five million were killed by 1953, and four to six million were sent to forced labor camps.[36]

In cities businesses were nationalized, but often with more limited bloodshed except for widespread executions of those considered to have been traitors or dangerous class enemies. From 1950 to 1953 China fought a costly war against the United States and its allies in Korea, and this set back progress, but by 1953, when it ended, Communist rule in China was well established and the danger of American intervention seemed removed. Following a Stalinist model, a new five-year plan prioritized heavy industry, not agriculture or consumer goods. The fact that Mao had relied on peasant support to win the Civil War did not make his a particularly peasant-friendly regime. Most land was still private, but the government extracted the food necessary to feed the cities by forcing peasants to sell produce at artificially low prices. Another important aspect of the institutions established was that people were labeled by their class origins; this status was passed on to their progeny, who would either benefit if they had the right class origins, or be subjected to limited education and work opportunities if they did not, in effect creating a kind of a caste system that would persist and create serious problems later in Mao's reign. A popular saying encapsulated this: "If the father's a hero, the son's a good chap; if the father's a reactionary, the son's a bad egg."[37]

In 1956 the "Hundred Flowers" campaign was launched. Intellectuals were urged to express complaints about Communist rule in order to find ways of accelerating progress and assuaging dissatisfaction. This was shut down in 1957 because Mao was surprised by the level of discontent. Three hundred thousand intellectuals were condemned as "rightists," many were exiled for life to labor camps or jails, and most of those spared had their careers ruined, robbing China of needed talent for a generation.[38]

By 1957 the Communist Party had created its governing institutions and stabilized politics, but economic progress was slow, so Mao was impatient to advance the revolution much faster to catch up with the West. By then, also, the Sino-Soviet alliance was breaking down and turning into active hostility because of Nikita Khrushchev's partial liberalization and anti-Stalinist measures. Mao thought it was time to show that China, not the backsliding Soviet Union, was the true revolutionary Marxist power.[39] That was when the Great Leap Forward was decreed in 1958.

Why have so many communist regimes, and revolutionary regimes in general, come to be dominated by a single charismatic leader, or at least one who does everything possible to make himself (the examples have all been men) seem godlike? The list is long: Lenin (who did not, however, live long enough to see what was done to his image after 1924), Stalin, Mao, Kim Il Sung, Ho Chi Minh, Tito, Castro, Ceaușescu, Hoxha, and many of their would-be socialist imitators in what has come to be called the Third World. For fascist leaders, this kind of deification is understandable because in typical fascist ideology the cult of the leader is central. Other revolutionary leaders, such as Mustafa Kemal "Atatürk" (father of the Turks), did the same. But nothing in Karl Marx's writing, or for that matter in Lenin's, recommends this. The answer, no doubt, is that revolutions that seek to completely replace an older set of institutions have no traditional legitimacy, and so fall back on the attempt to create a new form of monarchy with its own set of symbols, titles, and heroic legends (as did Napoleon too). And who will be the king? The leader of the party. But because the party cannot be questioned, its increasingly deified leader becomes officially untouchable. Did Marxist leaders actually believe that they had become infallible? Being given a dominant position in a ruthless party, having survived the violence that brought them to power, and being told by their followers that they were indeed the brain and heart of the party, they began believing it—after all, they were only human. Perhaps Stalin always understood that the cult of personality he encouraged was a way of legitimizing the rule of the Communist Party, but that he was not really infallible. Ho Chi Minh in Vietnam certainly knew this about himself. But Mao? By the late 1950s his successes had given him what Jonathan Spence has called a sense of quite unrealistic "euphoria." Other top leaders could use his charisma to consolidate their own power, and they were usually unwilling to contradict him. In a sense, whether Stalin, Mao, or any of the others really thought they were infallible is almost irrelevant. In states where terror and purges were a long tradition, and party loyalty was paramount, it eventually became dangerous to question the leader's omniscience. Those who did often paid dearly.[40]

The Great Leap Forward was based on Mao's firm belief that human will, mass enthusiasm, and collective organization could prevail over natural and human obstacles. Whether problems were due to water shortages, to limitations on how much could be grown on a given plot of land, to most people's selfish attachment to their families, to a shortage of technical expertise, or to almost anything else, Mao thought they could be overcome by firm ideological commitment to his particular interpretation of Marxist theory. He therefore pushed peasants into communes that separated them from their children and broke up families. Instead, there were communal canteens and living arrangements. Mao insisted that villages start producing iron and steel in order to hasten industrialization, and he decided that by very close sowing of seed China could grow a surplus of grain using only one-third of its land. In an August 1958 speech he said:[41]

> Yesterday I could not go to sleep. I have something to tell you . . . that a *mu* [1/6th of an acre, 0.0668 hectares] could produce ten thousand catties [6 metric tons] of grain [almost 90 tons per hectare—about 12 to 15 times what the most productive European grain producers get per hectare today, and more than 18 times what Japan manages]. I never dreamed it . . . I am afraid our 1.5 billion *mu* of farmland will be too much. Planting one-third of them is enough, another one-third may be turned to grassland, and let the remaining one-third be fallow. The whole country will then become a garden.

And as for the communes that were meant to destroy all traditional family ties and any individualism, Kang Sheng, perhaps Mao's most sinister, manipulative, and vicious henchman wrote, "Communism is paradise; / The people's communes are the bridge."[42] (Kang Sheng, it might be noted in passing, also provided Mao with pretty young women to satisfy his growing taste for his particular version of paradise.)[43]

It was an unmitigated disaster. Peasants melted down metal implements to fulfill iron production quotas, the communes were largely dysfunctional, agricultural production diminished drastically, and famine set in throughout large parts of China. But Mao's wishes continued to be brutally enforced, with obligatory procurement of grain that made it all worse. Tallying the numbers is tricky, but tens of millions were starved, beaten, or worked to death. Estimates of deaths vary from a low of fifteen million to a high of forty-five million. Yet even those who question the highest figures recognize this was an unprecedented, ideologically driven, and therefore unnecessary human tragedy that not only killed people but also precipitated enormous environmental damage. Mortality was especially concentrated in certain Central Chinese provinces and Sichuan. The death toll in some villages, according to Jonathan Spence, could reach a fifth to half of the population, particularly in Anhui Province.[44]

It was already evident by 1959 that this was a catastrophe, but Mao was unwilling to countenance opposition that might question his wisdom. When Peng Duhai—a senior veteran of the Long March, one of China's top generals who was then minister of defense—tried tactfully to get Mao to moderate his policy in 1959, he failed. Mao was enraged and had Peng disgraced and precluded from holding any office. Peng later died in prison. The Great Leap continued.[45]

Gradually, in 1961, some key party leaders, particularly Liu Shaoqi—a very trusted longtime Mao ally and now formally the president of China—began to back off and try to limit Mao's most radical policies. Mao seemed to accede, but he resented being sidelined and was sensitive to the growing opinion within the leadership that his sexual promiscuity and lavish lifestyle were improper. He began to line up his closest supporters to help him, including his fourth and last wife, Jian Qing. Lin Biao, one of the main generals who had led Communist armies to victory over the KMT in Manchuria, spoke of Mao's thoughts as "the pinnacle of Marxism Leninism." Lin was defense minister, so he was able to secure the People's Liberation Army as a crucial base by appointing Mao supporters to key positions. The longtime enforcer of Mao's purges, Kang Sheng, and Mao's favorite Marxist theoretician, Chen Boda, were reliable Maoists who were also enlisted.

In 1966 Mao struck, starting with some fairly obscure articles, but suddenly he had mass demonstrations erupt against the party hierarchy and bureaucracy. This was the Cultural Revolution. Troops of discontented youths, some but hardly all from previously undesirable families whose aspirations had been frustrated, formed "Red Guard" bands to attack all authority figures as being "insufficiently red." The Red Guards were encouraged to become vicious. One of their marching songs extolling the destruction of officialdom said, "Get lost! We're gonna chase you out of your fucking job! Kill! Kill! Kill!" When Red Guard violence got out of hand, however, they were disbanded in 1968. Still, the Cultural Revolution continued, and ultimately probably something on the order of a million more Chinese died, while twice that many wound up in forced labor camps.[46]

Top party leaders like Deng Xiaoping, another formerly very trusted Long March veteran who had tried to moderate Mao, were purged and publicly humiliated. Liu Shaoqi was purged in 1968 and then jailed. He died sick, abused, and unattended in his cell. Whole families were destroyed. Mao redoubled his policy of "learning from the masses," by which he meant following his own ideological inclinations that had become increasingly hostile to experts and intellectuals. Hundreds of thousands of youths were sent out to villages and deprived of the opportunity to get a higher education.

Lin Biao was designated as Mao's successor, but it seems that Mao began to fear a military coup and to see Lin as a potential Napoleon Bonaparte. The official story was that Lin and his family were plotting to overthrow Mao, but whether or not that was true, the upshot was that a rift opened up between Lin and Mao. Lin and his family fled in 1971, but their plane crashed, probably running out of fuel in Mongolia on the way to the Soviet Union. The Cultural Revolution was in a sense now disgraced, and though it was not over until Mao died in 1976, it began to be toned down. The ever-reliable Zhou Enlai, who had survived, started to bring back some measure of sanity to the situation, including starting to forge an alliance with the United States against the hated Soviet Union.

Ultimately, the shock of what had happened was so great that after Mao's death in 1976, within a couple of years Deng Xiaoping had gained control of the party. He began a long Thermidorian period of moderation that would open China to market forces and globalization to turn it from a chaotic, violent, dysfunctional society into the economic and political superpower it has become. Yet it remains to be seen whether Communist China can ever really rid itself of the consequences of having as its founding hero a monster, and whether Roderick MacFarquhar is right to say that something like the Cultural Revolution could possibly recur.[47]

Why Were Cambodia and Vietnam Different?
On the Diversity of Communist Regimes

Stalin wanted to create a modern, industrially advanced, militarily powerful socialist society, and he believed he was doing that. Mao long wanted the same for China, though ultimately, with the Cultural Revolution, he let his vanity and ideological fantasies push China in precisely the opposite direction. Almost all other communist states, whatever strategies they favored and failures they experienced, intended to be modernizers, building well-educated, rational, technological societies. Cambodia was a glaring exception.

Cambodian Communists (called Khmer Rouge, or Red Khmer) long fought to take over the country. They had been forced into remote rural areas that subsequently suffered heavily from American bombing during what Vietnam officially calls the "War of Resistance against America to Save the Country." (This is usually shortened to "Resistance War against America.") Many Khmer Rouge rural areas were near Vietnam and were being used by the North Vietnamese to bring supplies and men to South Vietnam. This phase of the war intensified after a 1970 coup in Cambodia by the right-wing military that overthrew the popular neutralist Cambodian Royal Government of Prince Norodom Sihanouk. Sihanouk then joined the Communists, who were able to recruit peasants who looked to them for protection from the bombing. They triumphed in 1975 after a long and terrible civil war. The Americans, having left in their wake enormous devastation, lost the long war against Communist North Vietnam and abandoned both their South Vietnamese and their Cambodian military allies. Communist Vietnam was united and Cambodia became Communist.[48]

What was unique about the Khmer Rouge was that they saw their future as an agrarian communal paradise that they would achieve by creating a socialist version of the medieval Khmer Empire. This program was based on a delusion reinforced by what French colonial historiography had concluded, that this empire had had a much more productive agriculture than did present-day Cambodia. More recent scholarship has shown this to be impossible; however, the Khmer Rouge leadership believed it. They planned to reproduce such imaginary wealth by dragooning the entire country, including Cambodia's large urban population, into intensive, hard rural labor, as they thought the rulers of the Khmer Empire had done. This time, however, it would be for the benefit of the poor ordinary peasants, not for an imperial elite. The ensuing mass enthusiasm and energy would then re-create Cambodia's imperial glory and even allow it to recapture territory lost over the centuries to neighboring Vietnam.

Instead, in four years of their rule they managed to cause the death of a larger proportion of their population than had any other communist revolutionary state.

The ideology that caused all this was not just the acceptance of a myth about the past, but also a combination of the twentieth century's most noxious political ideas. The Khmer Rouge's top leadership, Pol Pot, Nuon Chea, Khieu Samphan, and Ieng Sary, were guided less by original Marxism-Leninism than by admiration of Mao's most extreme policies. Of these four, it is worth noting, Nuon Chea was the only one who never studied in a French university. The others learned from leftist French intellectuals all too well, especially in French Communist publications. (Nuon Chea went to a Thai university.) Pol Pot would become "Brother Number One" in Angkar, the secretive organization of top party leaders. Nuon Chea was "Brother Number Two," and Ieng Sary "Number Three." Khieu Samphan, who had earned a PhD in Paris, was the titular head of the Khmer Rouge state. Pol Pot, while in Paris from 1949 to 1953, had read about the French Revolution, as well as some of Stalin's works, and he particularly liked the writing of Jean-Jacques Rousseau.[49]

Another essential leg of Khmer Rouge ideology was pure ethnocentric racism that was closer to fascist ideology than to anything Marxist. The leaders believed that the Khmer race had been polluted by both cultural and biological mongrelization, much as Hitler had posited about Germany's weakness. In the Cambodian case the first culprits were the Vietnamese, whose influence and physical presence had to be eliminated to purify the Khmer race. The second polluter was Western influence, so Cambodia had to be freed of all that was Western. That meant dispensing with modern technology, killing those with more advanced education, and eliminating all urban life because cities were irremediably polluted by foreign ways. It is revealing that Pol Pot (whose real name was Saloth Sar) had taken the pseudonym "Original Khmer" as author of an article he had written while studying in Paris.

Immediately upon winning power, the Khmer Rouge emptied cities, chiefly Phnom Penh, the capital bloated with refugees who had fled the war in the countryside. The entire country became a rural forced labor camp. Minorities, especially the Vietnamese still living there, and the mostly Muslim Chams, were slated for destruction. The Khmer Rouge claimed as their own territory the far south of Vietnam because that had once been part of the Khmer Empire, and they began to raid its border areas. They also concentrated the worst of their atrocities on Cambodia's southeast, the region that bordered on southern Vietnam. That was where they suspected there was the most mixing with Vietnamese bodies and ideas. These drastic measures were enforced by a predominantly very young group of recruits, sometimes even children separated from their families, who lorded it over and killed many of those they controlled.

Trying to vastly increase agricultural production with primitive means and an absurd goal of reproducing imagined medieval productivity only caused famine and disease. As Mao had done earlier during the Great Leap Forward, when faced with falling productivity, the Khmer leadership doubled down on repression and turned on the party itself rather than modifying its dystopian policies. It jailed tens of thousands of party members and horribly tortured them and their entire families before killing them.

The nightmare ended only when, driven by their warped sense of reality, the Khmer Rouge regime attacked the far more populated Vietnam. This was madness, as Vietnam was now united under its own

Communist Party and possessed a powerful army that had vanquished both the French colonialists and the Americans, and would later, in February 1979, successfully stand up to a Chinese border invasion. In January 1979 Vietnam invaded Cambodia and quite quickly overthrew the Khmer Rouge, who retreated back into guerrilla warfare that lasted until 1998.[50]

We can never know the exact number of Cambodians who perished, but a best estimate is that about 1.9 million extra deaths can be attributed to the Khmer Rouge's policies. Roughly half of those who perished were directly murdered, and the rest died as a result of the famine and disease provoked by Khmer Rouge policies. In only four years, almost one-quarter of the entire Cambodian population was lost.[51]

All Communist regimes killed enemies and set up prison camps for dissenters and real or potential "class enemies." All had purges within their Communist parties. This stemmed from their ideologies and their leaders' belief that preserving single-party rule was the only way to achieve their goals, so those who opposed them mortally endangered the ultimate achievement of socialist utopias. That said, the numbers killed and imprisoned varied substantially, and so did the amount of time this continued after the revolutions themselves, or, in the case of Eastern Europe, after the imposition of Communist rule by the Soviet Union between 1945 and 1948. The same is true of the intraparty purges that varied from relatively mild to brutally murderous. In all these, the Khmer Rouge stood at the most brutally extreme. Stalin's Soviet Union, Mao's China, and the Kim family's North Korea have also been terrible. So was Enver Hoxha's Albania. (Hoxha, like top Khmer Rouge leaders, also attended a French university and was proud of his knowledge of French culture and history. His stay in France preceded World War II.) What characterized these extreme cases was an overwhelming sense of paranoia and xenophobia on the part of their leaders, who saw enemies everywhere, including among their closest collaborators and even long-time friends.[52]

Yet when we compare Vietnam to Cambodia, the rather different outcome shows that all the conditions that predisposed the Khmer

Rouge to such murderous extremism cannot by themselves explain why so much higher a percentage died under them than in their even more war-torn neighbor.

Ho Chi Minh's Communist Party was not led by gentle agrarian reformers who believed in democracy. Ho was a veteran Comintern agent trained in Moscow and long active in China and Thailand before he returned to Vietnam to organize a guerrilla army during World War II. He declared Vietnam's independence from French colonial rule in 1945 but was forced to fight a long war against France. The French, like the Dutch, the Portuguese, and—in some but not all of their colonies—the British, completely failed to understand that the old colonialism was no longer sustainable. The Americans, fixated after 1948 on the threat of communism, financed the last phases of the French War in Vietnam and, after the French defeat in 1954, stepped in to try to sustain the new anticommunist South Vietnamese government. Ho's Communists took over North Vietnam. The North, allied with Communist insurgents in the South, then fought an increasingly deadly, destructive war against the South and the Americans. They finally won the Resistance War against America in 1975, ending three decades of constant armed conflict. In Vietnam, as in China, Russia, and Fidel Castro's Cuba, Communism's greatest successes occurred where they were better able than their defeated domestic foes to mobilize popular nationalist sentiments against foreign intervention.[53]

About 3.3 million Vietnamese died (on both sides, but the large majority on the Communist side) in the American phase of the war, and at least another million during the French War, for a total of over 4 million.[54] The devastating mortality among the Communist forces is movingly captured in personal stories of former soldiers interviewed in the 2017 documentary by Ken Burns and Lynn Novick, *The Vietnam War*. This proportionately ranks with the worst of the war death tolls in the many twentieth-century conflicts.

Without soft-pedaling the horrendous brutality of the Vietnamese Communists after they took control of North Vietnam in 1954, and in the South after their victory in 1975, or for that matter during the war itself, we can see that Vietnam did not have the kind of "auto-genocide" that occurred in Cambodia, the massacres conducted under Stalin, or the vast number of deaths attributable to Mao in China.

In July 1953, confident that they were winning, the Communists began to enforce land reform in areas they controlled in the North, and this intensified after their defeat of the French in 1954. They followed the Chinese model of dividing the rural population into landlords, rich peasants, middle peasants, and landless laborers, even where, as in the Red River Delta, there were few big landlords or rich peasants. Yet young cadres sent into the countryside to enforce the reform had to mount attacks against the supposed exploiters, and if they weren't there, they were invented, as had happened in the Soviet Union and China. It was brutal, particularly since at the same time the party also started to purge noncommunist nationalists who had been their allies and local party cadres who were deemed less trustworthy. There were the usual hate-filled campaigns in which class enemies, real or invented, were humiliated, beaten, and often killed. How many died? We are faced with the common problem: there are no reliable figures. Christopher Goscha cites a very conservative estimate of 5,000 to 15,000 executions but then describes outrages of such widespread intensity that this seems too low. In *The Black Book of Communism*, Jean-Louis Margolin writes that up to 50,000 were executed, 50,000 to 100,000 were imprisoned, and 86 percent of party cadres were purged. Both authors cite similar Vietnamese and French sources, though Goscha's are more up-to-date. If the high estimates are accepted, the proportions are similar to those in China's land reform during the early 1950s, but nowhere near what would happen later in China, much less in Cambodia. Taking a midpoint in the estimates would still make the period from 1954 to 1956 very deadly.

In November 1956 Ho Chi Minh and his leading general, the victor of Dien Bien Phu and the French War, Vo Nguyen Giap, admitted that the party had been wrong to push so hard, and though collectivization would continue, it would be done less viciously. There were moves within the party to strengthen the rule of law and allow for some dissent, and this was tolerated for a few years until unitary party rule was re-affirmed in 1959. What Ho did not do was what both Stalin and Mao had

done when doubts had arisen about the calamity of forced collectivization and the great Leap Forward. Ho did not counter doubts about collectivization policy with an attack against his detractors and massive,
deadly purges. Why did Communist North Vietnam choose to be more
moderate? It was not yet a Thermidorian reaction. That would come
much later. But it was better than it could have been. For one thing,
North Vietnam and South Vietnam's Communists were increasingly at
war with American-backed South Vietnam and needed a supportive
population.[55]

A second but unmeasurable factor might have been Ho Chi Minh's
own personality. The biographer William J. Duiker wrote of Ho that he
was "part Lenin and part Gandhi." He was educated as a Confucian as
well as in French, but even as a teenager he was an anticolonial nationalist. He was incredibly well traveled, multilingual, a founding member of
the French Communist Party, and a Comintern agent in Moscow,
China, and Thailand. Ho learned to navigate the dangerous shoals of
Soviet and Chinese Communist intrigues and intraparty struggles, always seeking a workable compromise. During World War II he fought
against the Japanese occupation of Indochina and worked with American intelligence agents. In 1945 and 1946 he offered the French a compromise that would have preserved their interests in Vietnam while allowing for eventual independence. France broke its promise to
compromise and launched a war to destroy the Communists. Later Ho
tried to compromise with the Americans too. Ruthless at times, and
willing to go along with the deification that turned him into an icon, he
evidently never believed he was infallible. We cannot know how much
that set the tone for the Vietnamese Communist Party, but it must
have had some effect in shaping a party in which, at least at the top, it
was possible to dissent without risking being purged and killed. There
was more, of course. After Khrushchev's 1956 speech denouncing Stalin and the emergence of the Sino-Soviet split, Ho worked hard to
remain neutral in order to keep the support of both, even though the
Chinese Communist leadership never trusted him or his top cadres
seeing them as too close to the Soviet Union. In the early 1960s, even
before his health began to deteriorate, Ho lost control of the party to

more hard-line leaders Le Duan and Le Duc Tho. He remained, however, a venerated, almost godlike official hero even as within the party he urged moderation and compromise. Yet he never tried to use his prestige to regain control. Instead, he remained dedicated to both his nationalist and communist goals and outward party unity.[56]

In a fascinating interview with a French reporter, shown on French television in June 1964, Ho was humorous, at ease, and his French, though a bit rusty, was still fluent. The French reporter said she was saddened to see that French cultural influence in North Vietnam had practically disappeared, and she wondered whether it could ever return. Smiling, Ho answered that French influence could never be what it once was, but Vietnam would be pleased to have normal relations with France as with other countries. He stressed that, despite the Sino-Soviet split, both Communist powers were firmly opposed to imperialism and supported his country. Only at the end of the interview did he suddenly show his emotional side. The reporter asked him if it was not true that North Vietnam was becoming a Chinese satellite. "JAMAIS!"—NEVER! he exclaimed.[57] The Americans never noticed that though he was a dedicated Communist, Ho was a true nationalist and obviously not China's puppet. Decades later, long after the end of the war, it has become obvious that Vietnamese public opinion is far more anti-Chinese than anti-American, despite the destruction the United States rained on their country.

Ho died in 1969. The Communists' conquest of South Vietnam in 1975, with Le Duan as the main leader, ushered in a new period of harshness. There was fear of a bloodbath, given massacres perpetrated by communist forces during the war—especially when they had occupied Hué for four weeks in 1968 during the Tet Offensive and executed some twenty-eight hundred captured South Vietnamese soldiers and civilians, many of them completely innocent.

There was no large-scale massacre, but a five-year plan following the Soviet model was instituted. It proved to be an economic disaster. Private enterprises were nationalized, hitting the large Sino-Vietnamese community in the South particularly hard. As the economy deteriorated, close to a million southern Vietnamese fled, mostly in perilously fragile, vulnerable boats. About two hundred thousand perished in the attempt. Most who succeeded wound up as refugees in the United States. In Vietnam, "re-education" in what were really harsh, prison-like brainwashing camps was imposed on higher-level officials and military officers of South Vietnam, though for lower-level ones, the re-education was milder and shorter. Unlike in Cambodia, there was no mass killing of South Vietnamese class enemies, though there was discrimination against them in educational and job opportunities. It was bad, and there were innumerable human tragedies, but given the Stalinist, Maoist, and Khmer Rouge examples, combined with the bitterness and huge death toll during thirty years of war, it could have been much worse.[58]

Already in 1979 some allowance was made for reopening markets in the south to provide food for Saigon (renamed Ho Chi Minh City, though to this day many residents still call it Saigon). More partial reforms were instituted until, in 1986, there was official recognition that strict state socialism was not working. Perhaps the death of hard-line leader Le Duan had something to do with this, though he was never the sole dictator that Stalin and Mao had been. The new policy was labeled *doi moi* (renovation) and opened Vietnam to the same kinds of capitalist reforms as those instituted a few years earlier in China by Deng Xiaoping. Vietnam reopened to the world and to private enterprise, but it remained firmly controlled by the Communist Party. This was, finally, the Thermidorian reaction after so much bloodshed and tragedy.[59]

All the elements that make for revolutionary radicalism and harshness were present in Vietnam. First there was the failure of liberal nationalism to sway the French enough to ease their colonial hold in the 1920s and 1930s. It is not only out-of-touch kings or emperors who fail to understand the level of popular discontent and the need to change. Colonial authorities have done so repeatedly, and the French were among the most stubbornly blind of all in the twentieth century. This was what gave Ho Chi Minh's Communists the chance to build up nationalist support and a solid base.[60] Then, three decades of war hardened the communists and made the struggle ever more tragically brutal. Finally, the triumph of a Communist Party with unrealizable utopian goals meant that after their victory, in order to attain those, they tried using use harsh repressive measures. Otherwise, their utopian goals would have had to be abandoned. But within these general parameters, the common elements in creating such catastrophic outcomes in many revolutions, there can still be significant variation. It is not whitewashing the Vietnamese Communist record to say that they did not, ultimately, take the path that Stalin took in the 1930s or that Mao took from 1958 through the Cultural Revolution. They took the path of moderating reforms instead of inflicting even greater pain. Vietnam did not become Cambodia, and for that it is better off today than it might have been. Though it remains a repressive one-party dictatorship, it has much private enterprise, and its people have far more personal freedom than they did before 1986.

Understanding the baleful consequences of so many revolutions is crucial if we are to learn anything at all from the past. But highlighting the differences, even between seemingly very similar cases, is equally important, because no generalized theoretical model can explain the variations caused by the personalities of leaders, by chance events, and by the international context in which each revolution has occurred.

5

Revolutions Betrayed

AUTOCRATIC CORRUPTION AND THE END OF IDEALISTIC THIRD WORLDISM

El que no transa no avanza. (He who isn't crooked doesn't get ahead)

—MEXICAN SAYING[1]

Chadli that's enough vice;
Tell your son to return the money.

—SLOGAN OF ALGERIAN YOUTHS PROTESTING PRESIDENT
CHADLI'S CORRUPTION IN RHYMING COUPLETS IN
COLLOQUIAL ARABIC, OCTOBER 1988[2]

THERE IS A STIRRING SCENE at the end of Gillo Pontecorvo's barely fictionalized film *Battle of Algiers* in which immense crowds come pouring out of the city's Arab quarter to demand independence on the occasion of French president Charles de Gaulle's December 1960 visit to Algeria when it was still a French possession. Such a mass demonstration really did happen and was a turning point. De Gaulle realized that Muslims, 90 percent of Algeria's population, were mostly loyal to the FLN (National Liberation Front) that had been fighting for independence since 1954. The demonstrations and ensuing street violence, pitting Muslims against the politically and economically dominant European settler minority, set in motion events leading to the negotiations that gave the FLN victory. Algeria became independent in 1962.[3]

In March 2003 when then French president Jacques Chirac visited Algiers, thousands turned out waving their passports and shouting, "Chirac, visa!" to demand the right to emigrate to France in order to find work. It was a sad symbol of the tragic failure of the Algerian revolution, and in a sense of Third Worldism as a whole.[4]

Third Worldism's Promises and Failures: Algeria, Angola, and Many Others

The term "Third World" was invented by French demographer Alfred Sauvy in a 1952 article in which he wrote, "Finally this Third World ignored, exploited, despised, like the Third Estate, also wants to be something." As former colonial societies that remained poor, stuck between the two hostile communist and capitalist other worlds competing for world domination, this Third World, Sauvy explained, was like the revolutionary French Third Estate in 1789 when the monarchy, church, and aristocracy had tried to marginalize it. Anyone familiar with French history would have recognized Sauvy's allusion to the Abbé Sieyès's words in his famous, influential 1789 pamphlet: "What is the Third Estate? Everything; What has it been politically until now? Nothing; What is it asking for? To be something."[5]

Sauvy's "Third World" immediately caught on and became the label for a loosely associated group of countries whose goal was to overturn the capitalist world system that had abused its colonies and presumably continued to keep them poor even after formal liberation. While socialist in its aspirations, the Third World sought also to stay free of Soviet domination. So Marshal Josip Broz Tito, communist dictator of Yugoslavia, became one of its inspirations because he had broken in 1948 with Stalin and gradually created a more open, somewhat more market-friendly kind of communism. Before Algerian independence, the other key leaders had been Gamal Abdel Nasser, the dictator of Egypt who had led the overthrow of Egypt's corrupt monarchy in 1952 and ended Britain's domination of his country, and Jawaharlal Nehru, Gandhi's disciple and the democratic socialist first leader of India who led it to independence from Britain in 1947. In 1962 newly independent Algeria joined as one of the most important members.

Algeria was central to Third Worldism. Its long, successful struggle against French colonialism and its aspiration to create a more just, economically developed socialist society were at the heart of what the Third World movement stood for. Its symbolic significance was even greater because it was in Algeria that a black French-trained psychiatrist from the French Caribbean island of Martinique had resigned from his work for the colonial authorities to join the FLN resistance. Frantz Fanon, who died of leukemia in 1961 at the age of thirty-six, had already published important books condemning white racism, the pernicious effects of which he had personally felt since his youth. Just before his death he published a book that became a landmark of left-wing anticolonial revolutionary literature, *The Wretched of the Earth*. In it he justified the use of violence to fight against colonial repression and racism. He also warned against elite takeover of newly liberated former colonies as a threat to the masses whom Third World governments were supposed to serve. Fanon called for international solidarity of oppressed people to create a better world.[6]

Had Fanon lived, what would he have thought of what befell the Algerian Revolution after its complete victory over France? And what about his hope that a new world system would emerge? None of it worked because Third Worldism became just another utopian mirage. As the idealism decayed, it then became an ideological excuse to justify many one-party, corrupt autocracies that may have begun as revolutionary anticolonial movements, but ceased to be once their elites were solidly in power.

In Algeria, as economic growth faltered and failed to provide nearly enough jobs for its growing youth population, protests erupted in 1988. These were violently repressed, and many young Algerians turned to radical religion as the only possible solution. In his 2004 foreword to *The Wretched of the Earth* Homi Bhabha wrote, "Fanon's best hopes for the Algerian Revolution were taken hostage and summarily executed, first by a bureaucratized military . . . and then by the

rise of fundamentalist groups like the FIS (Front Islamic du Salut—
Islamic Salvation Front)."[7]

Free Algeria was born with ample fertile land, very significant oil
reserves, and a good physical infrastructure. But even if it had had an
honest and efficient government, Algeria would have had a hard time
after it became independent in 1962.

Though France originally invaded Algeria in 1830, it took decades to
fully pacify the colony. European immigrants took over the best lands
and created prosperity for themselves, but Muslims were never granted
full citizenship rights or equal status, though many who obtained education did so in French. Algerians and denizens of other African French
colonies provided a significant proportion of the Free French Forces that
fought with Charles de Gaulle against the German occupation of France
from 1940 to 1944. But when Algerian Muslims demonstrated in 1945 to
gain a greater say and some measure of political equality, they were savagely repressed. After they began the revolt of 1954 that would lead to
independence, Algerians faced a long war in which the French used torture, aerial bombing of villages, and punitive raids that killed up to seven
hundred thousand out of a Muslim population of about ten million.
When the French left, the upper levels of the administration were left
entirely unstaffed, and there were too few qualified officials to take over.
European property was confiscated, but many enterprises and farms
could not be efficiently run. After the FLN took power, tens of thousands of Muslims who had worked with the French were slaughtered.
Also, independent Algeria was born with a significant ethno-linguistic
split between its Berber-speaking minority and the Arabic-speaking majority that dominated the FLN. There was, furthermore, a division between those who had fought and suffered within Algeria during the war,
and the well-equipped FLN army that had remained in Morocco and
Tunisia along their borders with Algeria. (Both Morocco and Tunisia
had been French colonies until they gained independence in 1956 without having to fight wars to gain it. Unlike Algeria, neither had many European settlers, and they thus had a different colonial status.)[8]

Algeria's first president, Ahmed Ben Bella, thought of himself as a
socialist Third World leader who would be able to bring about the kind

of modernizing, equitable society he dreamed of. In 1965 the army led by Houari Boumediène overthrew him and seized power. Boumediène's self-image mirrored Ben Bella's, but in effect from then on it was the military that called the shots, and that has reigned ever since.

Algeria adopted a Soviet-style model to develop heavy industry and rely on state-owned enterprises. As long as its major export, petroleum, fetched a high price, that policy was not an obvious failure, but oil prices fluctuated widely. The state-run economy was never efficient; it could not generate enough jobs to employ its rapidly growing population. By installing generally unqualified military men and their cronies in positions of wealth and power, the Algerian regime created a ruling class that would eventually fight tooth and nail to preserve its privileges. President Boumediène tried to control Islam but was unable to prevent the rise of radicals who could appeal to the discontented. By the time Boumediène died in 1978, Algeria's leadership in the Third World had become largely irrelevant. Various army cliques were fighting for power, all revolutionary impetus had been lost, and many Algerians sought to flee to France, the rich country whose language they spoke, where many other Algerians lived, and where job opportunities were far better.[9]

Unfortunately, corruption was built into the regime from the start. Without a transparent free press, and without a legitimate opposition to publicize abuse, the transgressions of the regime could not be questioned. Contracts with foreign firms, particularly but not only in the oil industry, involved bribes for the benefit of officials. The fewer jobs were available in the bloated bureaucracy and stagnant, inefficient economy, the more petty bribery and dishonesty spread throughout the society. The state-owned enterprises were granted monopolistic market positions, and money could be skimmed off by military officers and their allies. Ultimately, with that kind of widespread theft and massive inefficiency, Algeria no longer had enough oil money to pay off its unhappy population.

In 1991 the government tried to regain legitimacy by having elections, but when it became clear that the militantly Islamic party FIS would win, the elections were canceled. A vicious civil war broke out with massacres of whole villages, deadly reprisals by both sides, and widespread torture. As is usually the case, there is no adequate body count, but at least one hundred thousand died and many more were wounded. The worst of it was in 1993, but fighting continued until the late 1990s. At a great cost, what Mohammed Hachemaoui has called the "Pretorian regime" won. (Pretorian guards were originally supposed to protect Roman emperors, but they became powerful enough to make and undo emperors themselves.)[10]

Algeria has hardly been the only case of failed Third Worldism. Another dramatic example is Angola, whose ruling MPLA (People's Movement for the Liberation of Angola) began as a Marxist anticolonial revolutionary party led by Portuguese-educated African intellectuals. It fought a four-decades-long series of extremely bloody and destructive wars against the Portuguese, then against two other anticolonial but ethnically and regionally different movements. For much of the period after the Portuguese pulled out in 1974, the MPLA's main opponent was UNITA (National Union for the Total Independence of Angola), led by Jonas Savimbi, a man described to me, by a retired American diplomat who had some dealings with him, as a brilliant homicidal tyrant. The MPLA, led by José Eduardo dos Santos received major military support from Fidel Castro's Cuban army acting on behalf of the Soviet Union, because the Soviets viewed the ostensibly Marxist party as an ally in the Cold War. UNITA, just because it was opposed to the supposedly Communist MPLA, was helped by the United States, acting through its own proxy, apartheid South Africa. Only after the end of the Cold War and the transformation of South Africa did UNITA's support dwindle until finally UNITA was defeated and Savimbi was killed in 2002.

Angola, however, was never communist or even socialist except in the sense that the MPLA elite and dos Santos completely controlled Angola's huge oil reserves and used the national oil company as their private funding agency. The result was what Ricardo Soares de Oliveira calls "oligarchic capitalism, Angola style." Of course UNITA and Savimbi were no more defenders of democratic capitalism than the MPLA was genuinely Marxist. The Cold War struggle that occurred at Angola's expense made little ideological sense. The dos Santos regime never stopped selling oil to the West, the Soviets and Cubans gained nothing from their support of the MPLA, and the United States proved itself to be completely hypocritical in its alliance with apartheid South Africa and Savimbi—who, by the way, sometimes styled himself as a Maoist when he was not on fund-raising expeditions to the United States, where he presented himself as a good Christian defender of democracy.

With its oil-derived wealth, post–civil war Angola created a prosperous enclave economy centered in the capital city of Luanda. A small minority of privileged supporters garnered huge benefits and a lavish lifestyle, while the large majority of the population remained impoverished. Starting off with many strikes against it, Angola would at best have had a hard time creating a just, prosperous society. The centuries of Portuguese rule had depended on one of the worst and longest cases of slave raiding and trading. When that stopped, the Portuguese provided far too little educational or infrastructural development before departing. From the start Angola was ethnically deeply divided. Decades of civil war left the country ravaged and destitute. Nevertheless, with all that oil revenue, much more could have been done through either a market-friendly or a genuinely more socialist approach to economic development. Instead, the winning MPLA emerged from the war as a single ruling party with a well-developed military and repressive apparatus, such that its monopoly of power was almost impregnable, and corruption reigned unchecked. Angola became one of the most corrupt and unequal countries in the world.[11]

In 2017, after thirty-eight years in power, dos Santos retired and his family has been removed from power, but there is little sign that the ruling elite is prepared to change its ways. Rather, the recently announced anticorruption drive may be primarily intended to spread the wealth more evenly within the ruling elites that soured on the dos Santos clan because it was raking off too much money for itself. Before the change, dos Santos's daughter was reputed to be the wealthiest woman in Africa.[12]

The many other cases of failed Third World idealism that descended into corruption, coups, economic failures, and civil wars show that it was not just idiosyncratic failures that led to Algeria's and Angola's failures, but something more systemic. By the 1980s, not much was left of the original vision.[13]

Why? Trying to develop an economy where the most important sectors are controlled by the state inevitably means creating a large bureaucracy. The Soviet Union tried to substitute in the place of market incentives quotas and bonuses for those who performed well, and under Stalin there was always the threat of arrest, even execution for those who did not. But if this was for a time an effective strategy to make the Soviet Union an industrial-military great power, in the long run it could never overcome the problems of central planning that was unable to measure supply and demand adequately. After Stalin's death the terror mostly receded. Once bureaucrats running an economy are no longer threatened with removal for poor performance, and if on top of that they are inadequately paid, the path is open not only to growing inefficiency but also to corrupt practices that begin to infect all public services. If, furthermore, there is a ruling party that tolerates no dissent or opposition, the ruling elite almost inevitably learns that it can take advantage of its power to enrich itself even if the economy deteriorates and the mass of the population suffers.[14]

Finally, in the case of Algeria and many other Africa and Asian countries, birthrates remained high for most of the twentieth century (and still are in sub-Saharan Africa) even as rudimentary health services lowered infant mortality, so the population grew rapidly. The demographic surge has left an ever-growing percentage of the young population with few job prospects, decaying and inadequate educational institutions, and a pervasive sense of frustrated anger.[15] In other words, the Third World economic model as it was practiced in Algeria had almost no chance of success. If unbridled capitalism left poor countries that relied on a few mineral and agricultural exports vulnerable to price swings and exploitation by the most powerful capitalist nations, the Algerian model and others like it were no better.[16]

In one way or another, the Algerian story has been repeated for most of the Third World socialist or semisocialist revolutionary regimes. Kwame Nkrumah's Ghana, Sékou Touré's Guinea, Robert Mugabe's Zimbabwe, Gamal Abdel Nasser's Egypt, Hafez al-Assad's Syria, Muammar Qaddafi's Libya, and others followed similar paths: idealistic revolutionary goals, state-centered economic development that claimed to follow a socialist model, one-party dictatorship, bureaucratic and elite corruption, growing repression as the economy failed to develop fast enough, and the collapse of the original idealism. All the Arab republics born of anticolonial revolutions became corrupt autocracies. So did most of sub-Saharan Africa.

It was precisely these conditions—deep-seated corruption spreading from the top to lower levels and making every aspect of daily life unfair—that triggered the so-called Arab Spring of 2010–2011. It all began with the suicide of a small-town street vendor in Tunisia who could no longer bear the constant humiliation imposed by the local authorities and their demands for bribes. From there it spread, though almost everywhere outside Tunisia the push for revolutionary reforms led to violence and ultimately failed.[17]

I am not suggesting that major corruption happens only in regimes that have claimed to be revolutionary socialists. In Africa the problem is so pervasive that such a conclusion is obviously unwarranted. Three of the worst cases are Nigeria, the Democratic Republic of the Congo, and Equatorial Guinea, none of which have ever tried to implement a revolutionary leftist orientation.[18]

Nor is Africa unique, though it has a disproportionate number of the world's most corrupt countries. High levels of damaging corruption exist in much of Asia and Latin America, though there the very worst case is also the supposedly revolutionary "Bolivarian" Venezuela.[19]

What began as truly reformist, idealistic revolutionary movements ultimately degenerated badly, and what is most disturbing about this is that they once held out real promise of something cleaner. Few expect any better from countries dominated by autocratic, rich elites such as the landowning classes that for so long ruled many Latin American countries. Nor is the power of corrupt money absent in democracies, though at least those have the possibility of exposing and countering that kind of dishonest manipulation of power. Revolutions promised more than this, and their very common failures have left much of the world looking for different solutions that rely on religious traditionalism or a reversion to ethnic tribalism. That is the tragedy of failed Third Worldism: not only did the original promises fail, but the consequences of that failure have created even worse outcomes.

A final case that holds a warning is the story of what happened to Russia after the collapse of the Communist Soviet Union.

European Communism's Collapse and Russia's Path from Lenin to Putin's State

Corruption in the Soviet Union and the Eastern European communist states was not the same as in kleptocratic states like Angola. Nor was it like what happened in dictatorships like Algeria's where a small military elite effectively plundered the country's resources.

Naturally the Communist Party elites lived much better than the masses, but by and large not that extravagantly. When I visited the principal home of Romania's former Communist dictator, Nicolae Ceaușescu, a year after his 1989 execution, I saw it was very nice, but no more luxurious than many homes of rich Americans and Europeans. Ceaușescu ruined Romania with his policies and some extravagant public building projects, not by stealing resources for personal use.[20] Most top party people in his country lived no better than typical upper-middle-class or even just plainly middle-class Americans. The same was true in the Soviet Union and elsewhere in Eastern Europe. The corruption in those countries was fundamentally destructive, but not because of open kleptocracy by a tiny number of power holders.

As the Hungarian economist János Kornai has extensively explained, the communist economic systems invariably produced shortages, not only in material goods but in essential services like health care, house or apartment maintenance, and even access to higher education. So it became common practice to bribe doctors and nurses, educators, plumbers, those who issued licenses or permits, and so on. Service personnel were systematically underpaid, spare parts were never produced in sufficient quantities, and far too much money was wasted on big industrial projects that ran at what would have been seen as a loss in more market-driven economies. Perhaps even more corrosive, the very state enterprises that were considered important often had to bribe or exchange favors with other enterprises to get essential raw materials, machinery, and spare parts. In other words, corruption was baked into the system so thoroughly that it became essential for both personal and national economic survival. What was unusual in communist states was that the corruption was less a function of a deliberately exploitative, thieving elite that starved the general economy by its dishonesty than it was the essence of the system itself. Avoiding corruption was impossible because without it the society could not function.[21]

In the Soviet Union and in Eastern Europe the governing classes were well aware of what was going on, and as time went on, they increasingly closed their eyes to the problem.[22] A whole class of illegal entrepreneurs and black marketers arose to take advantage of the system by providing essential services. The security services and other party officials not only knew what was going on but increasingly participated. This kind of generalized cynicism caused even somewhat privileged Communist Party members to lose faith in the legitimacy of their system, and ultimately badly weakened their regimes.[23]

So when the communist system fell in Eastern Europe in 1989 and in the Soviet Union in 1991, it turned out that there were clever individuals already well versed in trading and providing key services, and therefore ready to take advantage of the drive to privatize the entire economy. Because the Soviet Union had been communist decades longer than its onetime Eastern European satellites, the inherently corrupt system was more deeply rooted. After 1991 a new class of what are called "oligarchs" emerged. Working with and consisting partly of former KGB intelligence agents, established fixers, criminal organizations, and certain well-placed party officials, this new class became the ultrawealthy owners of key enterprises as they were privatized.

In Russia some members of the old ruling party apparatus, and particularly key KGB operatives, took power, enriched themselves, and created a new, more corrupt, more nakedly kleptocratic system than the one that had existed before. Markets now were allowed to play a major role, so shortages were greatly alleviated, but the new elites also entered into closer cooperation with the Russian mafia, whose hit men were used as enforcers and murderers in the competition for power and money. In fact, distinctions between the FSB (Federal Security Service—the new name for the old KGB), the oligarchs, and the Russian mafia became hard to discern. As Karen Dawisha so comprehensively documented, at the top of this there now sits former KGB agent Vladimir Vladimirovich Putin. He not only presides over a very corrupt Russia, but is working hard to influence and spread that corruption to as much of the capitalist West as possible.[24]

Not surprisingly, Russia is listed as the 43rd most corrupt (out of 180 countries) in the world by Transparency International (tied with Mexico). Most other former Soviet republics that are now independent have also succumbed to similar forces. Ukraine, the 61st most corrupt, is the most populous of these after Russia. The so-called Ukrainian Orange Revolution of 2004 and the Maidan Revolution ten years later, which were supposed to give birth to democracy and reform, turned out to do nothing of the sort and hardly qualify as "revolutions" except in the eyes of hopeful Westerners who should know better.[25] All of the Central Asian republics also rank high in the corruption index (see note 19 to this chapter and note 10 to chapter 6 for the references).

How much of the current state of affairs in Russia, Ukraine, and Central Asia is a cultural legacy that predates communism? Is the widespread corruption primarily the holdover of communism itself? The Russian Empire before the Bolshevik Revolution was hardly free of corruption, but in the Soviet Union that problem became more deeply ingrained. And Russia, alone among the postcommunist states, has created a powerful autocratic regime that is not only corrupt and murderous, but also capable of using its mafia, its very rich oligarchs, and its security services in tandem to influence and disrupt other states, even strongly democratic ones. That aspect is very much part of the Soviet legacy and its onetime revolutionary ambitions to spread communism everywhere. Now it is sleaze, graft, and lies that it spreads to enhance its international power, not the earlier idealistic (if deeply flawed) message of universal equality through socialism. In only one century this has been the final legacy of Lenin and Stalin. Neither they nor the millions of their onetime idealistic admirers ever envisioned such an outcome.

So has it been with too many revolutions as it has been in Russia from the early twentieth century to the early twenty-first: stubborn resistance to change by the old regime, followed by the failure of liberal reforms, the triumph of radical revolution that imposed brutal policies to force change, autocracy, and eventually a slow slide into corruption. All the original idealism and hope that produced and justified such bloody sacrifices turned out to have been for naught.

6

Peaceful Revolutions?

INTERPRETING CONSERVATIVE AND LIBERAL SUCCESSES AND FAILURES

As the world marks the centenary of the October Revolution, Russia is once again under the rule of the tsar

—FRONT COVER PICTURE OF THE
ECONOMIST ON OCTOBER 26, 2017[1]

If we want things to stay as they are, things will have to change.

—GIUSEPPE TOMASI DE LAMPEDUSA IN HIS NOVEL,
THE LEOPARD (IL GATTOPARDO) PUBLISHED IN 1958)[2]

ARE ALL REVOLUTIONS that terrible? Of course not. There have been revolutions that avoided massive bloodshed even if there was some violence. There have been moderate ones that produced neither repressive autocracy nor thorough corruption.

In the second half of the nineteenth century, Germany and Japan went through major changes that turned out to be genuinely revolutionary, but they were guided by socially conservative leaders who understood that progressive reforms were necessary to avoid more dangerous outcomes. Still, these two cases can illustrate the dangers of overly conservative transformative regimes.

The more obviously revolutionary upheavals in the Eastern European communist states in 1989 were even more dramatic examples because they were largely nonviolent and not led by conservatives. Entire economic and political regimes ended abruptly and were replaced by liberal, capitalist democracies. The same seemed to happen to the Soviet Union in 1991. But as we will see, in the longer run, even the most seemingly benign revolutions may not eventually turn out to be quite what they seemed.

There have also been societies able to accommodate truly revolutionary social, political, and economic changes without revolutions at all. The United Kingdom managed this very successfully from the late eighteenth century to the twentieth. Given flexible institutions and mostly reasonable elites willing to countenance change, industrialization can be managed gradually without a revolutionary break at all. But as we have seen, lacking such good fortune, adapting to modernizing change is difficult and often leads to disastrous upheavals.

Two Flawed Conservative Revolutions:
Bismarckian Germany and Meiji Japan

It might be considered oxymoronic to call crucial but conservative political transformations revolutionary, but there are examples that conform to the famous quote from Lampedusa's novel *The Leopard*, cited above. In the second half of the nineteenth century socially and culturally conservative German and Japanese governments led necessary changes that headed off more radical outcomes. Most of the French court and aristocracy in 1788 and 1789, like China's rulers in the late nineteenth and early twentieth centuries, failed to understand how necessary this was, and they paid a steep price for being shortsighted.

In 1848 there was a failed German liberal revolution. Reactionary antiliberals remained in power, particularly in the most important German state, Prussia. Subsequently, however, led by a very conservative but flexible Prussian government headed by Otto von Bismarck, Prussia united the various German states and adapted very well to a changing world. By the start of the twentieth century it was allowing much more democracy, gradually incorporating the working class as it had earlier permitted the middle classes to have a political voice, and its scientific research institutions were the strongest in Europe. Germany had the most progressive and largest economy in the world after the United States. The tragedy was that Germany's political and military elites then lost sight of the fact that their country's political stability and economic success were based on adapting to social change, promoting education, and supporting scientific and technical research. Instead, they came to believe that Germany's success was due to its victorious wars of 1864, 1866, and 1871, and to aggressive Prussian militarism. Germany then sought to use its advantages to engage in the nationalist fever and imperialist ambitions that were destabilizing Europe. It was the ensuing world war that prepared the way for the much more drastically radical rise of Nazism.[3]

Japan's transformation after what was called the "Meiji Restoration" of 1867–1868 was even more revolutionary than Germany's, but in some ways more culturally conservative as well. Japan was turned into a major modern power in three decades. Before the restoration there had been economic progress and a relatively high literacy rate. There were protests and social disruptions directed against the old regime, so it was not simply the threat of foreign intervention that brought down the Tokugawa Shogunate that had ruled since the early seventeenth century. Yet that perception of immediate danger from Western powers precipitated the coup of 1867 and the political changes of 1868. There followed a whole series of truly revolutionary transformations. The reforms were carried out by enlightened, socially conservative bureaucrats, not by radicals intent on overthrowing the entire social order. It is not surprising, then, that Japanese bureaucrat-intellectuals specifically looked at the social reforms promulgated by Bismarck's Germany to limit social disruptions and try to prevent the rise of socialism. There was some violent resistance to the 1867 political coup, but after that was brought under control, what followed was gradual change over several decades. Japan industrialized and created a powerful, modern military. It westernized its legal and educational institutions, and adopted a constitutional monarchy. By pretending to "restore" imperial power, which had been sidelined for centuries, the Meiji Restoration actually created something new while maintaining conservative social and cultural norms. So did Japan have a real revolution? Yes, and as Carol Gluck and others have pointed out, the restoration had one thing in common with more radical revolutions, especially the French one, in that it marked an "epochal dividing mark between the past and the present."[4] As with Germany, sadly, Japan also used its economic success to turn itself into an aggressive imperial power, and that led to the tragic outcome of its wars from 1931 to 1945 that came close to destroying it.

It hardly needs to be pointed out that this was the dark side of the German and Japanese conservative, gradual, moderate kinds of revolutionary change. They left socially reactionary classes with too much power and a tradition of aristocratic militarism that propelled their nations into calamitous aggression.

Though most Americans might not recognize this, the pandering to conservative slave-owning elites in the South when the United States was established also had nefarious long-term consequences, not only the great Civil War of 1861–1865, but a persistent conflict about race that continues to plague the country to this day.

A Liberal Success? The Fall of European Communism and the Disappointing Aftermath

When in 1989 communism disintegrated throughout Eastern Europe (except in Albania, where it happened in 1991), its legitimacy had been eroding for years. Corruption was omnipresent and reviled. Economic stagnation had soured the promise of rapidly rising material comfort. Greater opening to Western Europe had highlighted the poor economic performance of the communist states and also trapped most of them into increasingly unsustainable debts incurred to those Western countries. The personal freedoms available in noncommunist Europe made the repressive dictatorships in the communist ones seem even more onerous despite the fact that generally the situation was not as bad as it had been during the Stalinist period from 1948 to 1953. The Soviet Union was suffering from the same problems and had the added burden of paying for its costly arms race with the United States. When the Soviet reformist leader Mikhail Sergeyevich Gorbachev announced that his country would no longer intervene in the politics of its former Eastern European satellites, what had seemed to be solidly entrenched if troubled regimes suddenly collapsed.[5]

In Romania somewhat over two thousand were killed, but there was remarkably little violence in Poland, Hungary, East Germany, Czechoslovakia, and Bulgaria. Even in Romania, a majority of the deaths were attributable to chaotic misunderstandings and panic rather than anything close to a civil war. Compared to the major revolutions we have looked at in this book, 1989 was amazingly conflict free because the ruling elites did practically nothing to save communism. Yet what happened in Eastern Europe were real revolutions that upended entire economic and political orders that had been in place for four decades and had seemed, only a few years earlier, to be secure because of their effective repressive institutions. Eastern Europe then transitioned into more or less democratic, liberal regimes.[6]

Yugoslavia, with its looser, more liberal form of communism, should have had an easier transition away from its old regime, but it did not, and instead almost immediately fell into a bloody set of ethno-religious civil wars with hundreds of thousands of deaths and millions of refugees. Yugoslavia is therefore not recognized as another example of the fairly benign revolutionary outcomes the rest of the region experienced. It was, in an unfortunate way, an example of a failed liberal revolution that reverted to its immediate pre-1945 past, especially the deadly civil wars that accompanied the World War II occupation of the country by Germany and Italy.[7]

Two decades later, however, it began to be apparent that the peaceful, liberal revolutions of 1989 might not have such happy long-term outcomes. Instead, ethnic nationalism and antidemocratic populism have reared their heads, most obviously in Poland and Hungary. Is it that moderate revolutions leave unresolved problems that emerge only later, or is it an entirely different, worldwide antiliberal trend at work?[8]

The answer to that question is that no revolution can ever solve all a society's problems or eradicate all baleful legacies of the past. It has undoubtedly been better for Eastern Europe that aside from Yugoslavia, the gentle fall of communism spared countless lives and averted trage-dies that would have occurred if their revolutions had been radical and violent, or if the communist regimes had tried to suppress them. But all revolutions, even the relatively benign ones, are flawed and usually wind up disappointing their most idealistic supporters, be they extremist radicals or moderates.

As the Soviet Union disintegrated in 1991, there were deaths, but most were the result of long-standing ethnic conflicts, primarily in the Caucasus. Casualties were not caused primarily by government re-pression or a civil war between revolutionaries and the government. The Soviet Union, the world's second strongest great power, broke into fifteen separate republics. Russia, the dominant heartland of the Soviet Union, remained by far the biggest and most powerful of these, but its boundaries and population were greatly reduced. In the 1990s Russia appeared to transform itself into a liberal democracy; but as was discussed at the end of the preceding chapter, this never actually happened.

At the start of the twenty-first century, Russia began to try to regain some of its former power. Wars and violent ethnic conflict erupted along Russia's borders and in many of the new republics, almost all of which became corrupt autocracies or, at best, chaotically unstable. Only the three tiny Baltic republics—Estonia, Latvia, and Lithuania—are exceptions.

So yes, the Soviet Union also experienced a mostly peaceful politi-cal revolution that ended the communist economic system, but in the longer run it would be difficult to say that Russia achieved the kind of democratic capitalist society that the first wave of reformers had hoped for. Instead, it has in some ways reverted to the most noxious of both its tsarist and Soviet traditions. Today's Russia is an autocracy dominated by members of the former Soviet KGB. Vladimir Putin has used traditional tsarist Orthodox religiosity to bolster his legitimacy, and both tsarist and Soviet imperial pretensions to win over national-ists. The symbolism may be appealing to many Russians, but past gran-deur cannot easily be recaptured. Instead, there is likely to be future, unanticipated chaos, as demonstrations in Russia demanding a moderate democracy have been successfully repressed so that necessary reform has become increasingly unlikely.[9]

Nor are conditions much better in most of the rest of the former Soviet Union. In those new republics also there have been periodic outbursts of protest calling for more democracy and less corruption, the so-called color revolutions in Ukraine and some of the Central Asian republics that were hardly revolutionary at all. Whether in Ukraine or elsewhere, the supposed "revolutions" have accomplished little except for occasional changes in the leadership. In Central Asia such episodes have typically been manipulated by competing parts of the corrupt elite but with little real reform.[10]

Liberals were, as is so often the case, naive about their prospects in the early 1990s, but there were no radical revolutionaries to replace them, so instead some of the uglier aspects of the past—ethnic hatreds and crude nationalism, corruption, and autocracy—reasserted themselves. One day, eventually, some form of radicalism will emerge. It may be religious, especially in Muslim parts of the former Soviet Union. It might be a new form of fascism. Or there could be a new kind of far left. It will not be pretty.

In contrast to the once-promising, but subsequently more problematic revolutionary changes in European communist countries, let us briefly consider why in Asia, as in Cuba, communist regimes survived, though almost all of them, with the possible exception of North Korea, did undergo important reforms allowing more market forces to shape their economies. The long and short of it is that by being flexible enough to allow economic liberalization, most of these regimes, very notably China and Vietnam, presided over a major enhancement in their people's standard of living. Equally important, having seen what happened to European communism, the elites in the surviving communist states stuck together to defend their political systems so as to hold on to their power and privileges.[11]

If so, what about North Korea, which might seem to be the kind of incompetent regime destined to be overthrown as it remains mired in repression and poverty? The reality is that incompetent regimes have not always or even mostly produced revolutionary situations. As long as powerful elites do not abandon the system, they and the regime that they support can remain in power for very long periods of time even if the general welfare suffers. Communist North Korea has remained firmly in the grip of Kim Il Sung, his son, and grandson even as the country's economy has gone through periods of severe famine and deprivation. Isolated, viciously autocratic, and weakened by bad policies, the regime has nevertheless kept itself in power, and a small, privileged elite supports it, knowing—as the French aristocracy in 1788, the Russian elite in 1916, and the rising Iranian middle and professional classes in 1978 did not—that to abandon the ruling dynasty would almost certainly mean their own bloody doom. Furthermore, as Andrei Lankov has shown, the Kim family has been highly competent in maneuvering internationally and domestically to keep itself in power, so calling it incompetent or, as some have, irrational misses the point. North Korea is an abject failure in that it has not created anything remotely close to the utopia it promised its people, but a brilliant success in having survived in a difficult international environment and made life quite tolerable for its elite. So no revolution has occurred.[12] All that could change, of course, if the elite loses complete faith in the regime and decides that it could survive its overthrow. That is what happened in Communist Eastern Europe in 1989 and in the Soviet Union in 1991. There is no guarantee that it will never happen in North Korea, but so far it hasn't.

Is Adapting to Modernity without Revolution Possible? Yes, but . . .

Between the Glorious Revolution of 1688 and the late twentieth century, England changed completely. A country run by a small landed elite became a democracy in which the large majority of inhabitants, male and female, rich and poor, well educated or not, got the right to vote. It was transformed from an overwhelmingly agrarian society into a mostly urban industrial one, and then into an economy dominated by its service sector. The British have retained some quaint trappings of their past that they seem to cherish: among them the monarchy, wigs in law courts, and some of the ceremonies associated with Parliament. Aside from these purely symbolic remnants and some old buildings, a late seventeenth-century Englishman magically set down in modern London three centuries later would recognize almost nothing. Yet after 1688, unlike France or many other societies that went through the same immense changes, England had no new successful revolutions. The Industrial Revolution changed everything, but slowly enough so that the philosopher-economist Adam Smith, who is credited as the father of modern economics, did not even realize it was getting under way when he published *The Wealth of Nations* in 1776. There were violent protest movements, there were threats of revolution, but the remarkable thing about Great Britain was that its institutions and elites proved flexible enough to adapt before that went too far, except in Catholic Ireland, which was treated as an exploited colony. There is no need to sugarcoat the inequalities, repression of protests, military imperialism, or other unpleasant aspects of Victorian Britain to recognize that on the whole it handled its modernization better than France had.[13]

England may have been the first industrial nation, but massive transformation of the same sort then spread widely. Modernization does not require a political revolution as long as governments and dominant classes are willing to countenance gradual changes that are revolutionary in the long run, but do not seem to be except in retrospect. Unfortunately, all too often that does not happen, or happens in a way that leads to later disasters.

7

Are There Lessons for Us to Learn?

The mixture we now see of unbridled and irrational authority, of
rationalized technology and demagogic propaganda, presents a
caricature of the kind of inhumane society that could come about. The
decline of democratic institutions, the crisis of capitalist economies . . .
together with the degeneration of traditional values, culminate in the
present situation, where everything remains to be done because
everything is called into question.

—RAYMOND ARON IN 1939[1]

Those who make peaceful revolutions impossible will make violent
revolutions inevitable.

—JOHN F. KENNEDY IN 1962[2]

PRESIDENT KENNEDY LEFT A MEMORY of what an ideal liberal president should be, though his soaring rhetoric was not always matched by
actual accomplishments. Were he alive today, he would undoubtedly be
shocked by the level to which American politics have descended in recent decades, and also by the general decline of democracy in much of
the world. Raymond Aron might not be. From World War II until his
death in 1983, Aron was probably France's leading liberal intellectual (in
the more classical, moderate European sense as is defined in the next
paragraph below). Having witnessed the polarization and debasement

of Europe's democratic politics in the 1930s, he understood what that could lead to. His essay is as relevant today as it was in 1939.

We are returning to a pre–World War II world of unbridgeable polarization and doubts about the foundational ideals of democratic liberalism. What are those basic ideals that are under threat today, as they were in the late 1930s? They have five principal aspects.

1. A respect for individual human rights that still recognizes human variability
2. A belief in the capacity of democratic but not excessive government institutions to find solutions for major problems
3. Faith in the capacity of market economies with suitable limits and controls to deliver healthy outcomes that help the large majority of people without trying to enforce radical equality
4. Confidence that better education and the search for knowledge are essential
5. And, finally, a conviction that necessary reforms should nevertheless remain respectful of the best traditions and institutions that create a sense of solidarity and mutual respect between members of any nation

The French Revolution started off with these ideals, though in the late eighteenth century there was as yet little appreciation of what might happen if extremists came to power. The first half of the twentieth century saw both fascist and communist revolutions that utterly rejected liberal moderation. As we know, the end of the century appeared to many of us to mark a kind of ultimate triumph of liberalism, but that quickly turned out to be a vain hope. The opposite is happening as even in the democratic West there is a turn against the Enlightenment tradition that was long the basis of American and European democracy.

We may not be there yet, but Benjamin Carter Hett's analysis of the rise of the Nazis sounds almost as if it were written about today when he points out that "the rejection of rationality went hand in hand with the rejection of the liberal, capitalist West."[3] So did the constant lying, the contempt for the law, and the call to violence.

Today's seeming paralysis of liberal democracy also brings to mind Mancur Olson's prescient book, which is even more relevant today than when it was first published, *The Rise and Decline of Nations.*[4] Olson argued that over time powerful interest groups grow stronger and defend their wealth and privileges by blocking essential change and innovation. Only a rude shock, at worst a catastrophe, can unfreeze the resulting political and economic stagnation. This insight is useful in explaining the first of the eight main conclusions of our own study of revolutions.

CONCLUSION ONE. As we have seen in all of the revolutionary episodes, a kind of "Olson blockage" had occurred. States' political institutions solidified and became encrusted as those with power protected themselves by preventing reforms that risked endangering their wealth and privileges. That did not prevent social and economic change from occurring, as technologies, ideas, population size, the international environment, the natural environment, and many other conditions varied over time, but it did prevent the necessary political reforms from being carried out. Eventually the ensuing crises shook old systems loose. But unfortunately, when unresolved crises turned into revolutions, the potential for a catastrophic outcome rather than a peaceful set of reforms rose rapidly.

CONCLUSION TWO. It is possible to overcome a crisis if there are strong institutions that can be used by a self-aware political elite capable of understanding that change is necessary. England had these in the late eighteenth and nineteenth centuries. France in 1788, like Russia in 1917 or Iran in 1978, did not. In the absence of these two requirements, there is inadequate reform, and the probability of eventual revolution rises dramatically because social changes that come with economic and cultural modernization require political adaptation as well. War or severe economic downturns obviously increase that probability as the failure to reform hurts ever-larger numbers of people.

Are there dangerous prerevolutionary situations in today's turbulent world? Perhaps not yet in the democracies, though even in the United States and much of Western Europe there is growing political paralysis and an inability to pursue necessary changes. That is creating fertile ground for extremism that could eventually lead to unexpected upheavals. In much of the rest of the globe, especially in the Middle East, in Central and South Asia, and in parts of Africa and Latin America, the situation is more explosive. Russia and China, aside from their problems with corruption and a drift back into totalitarianism, have become almost classic fascist powers: militarily aggressive, nursing a bitter sense of grievance against Western democracies, and resolutely hostile to liberalism. As we have seen, important parts of formerly communist Eastern Europe are on the same track to illiberal autocracy. It is impossible to predict where disaster will strike next, but plausible to say that it will happen somewhere sooner or later in a way that could have dramatically bad results. (See Conclusion Three and note 5 below.)

CONCLUSION THREE. Most commonly in the early stages of modern revolutions moderate liberals come to the fore, but as was explained at the start of the book, the "La Fayette syndrome" is likely to marginalize them. In the dire circumstances of institutional collapse under the strains of wars, violence, and social disruption, liberals tend to underestimate both the anger of previously powerless masses and the growing appeal of those who propose radical solutions. That was why Condorcet, for all his brilliance and early popularity, fell victim to the radicals, as earlier had happened to La Fayette. Kerensky's fate in Russia in 1917 was the same, and, under different but partly analogous conditions, so was Shapour Bakhtiar's in Iran in 1979. These were not just individual failings. Liberal movements in general, like the Kadets in Russia, never quite understand how quickly revolutions that begin as relatively moderate demands for reform can spin out of control. Nor did Francisco Madero fully grasp the depth of desires by peasants and workers for more reform than he was willing to countenance. Madero also failed to see the great danger posed by the reactionary opponents of the Mexican Revolution. Die-hard conservatives conflate moderate reform that threatens their interests with far more dangerous radicalism that wants to exterminate them, and therefore are willing to turn to violent repression to stop necessary change. That is what happened in most very early revolutionary situations, thus making it more likely that extremists would take over.

Reading about the shocked reaction of European and American liberals to rising populist anger in their own countries is a good reminder that something analogous is starting to happen in the Western democracies. Why this is happening has been well analyzed by others and is not within the purview of this book. Nevertheless, we can see some distressing similarities with past liberal failings, and we may wonder whether we are fated to see something similar.[5] This is why studying the next stage that occurred when liberal reform failed and led to revolution is both instructive and alarming.

CONCLUSION FOUR. It is not just moderate liberals who lose control because they do not fully grasp what very radical extremists have in mind. Conservative German politicians brought Hitler to power because they considered an alliance with the Nazis preferable to making compromises with the very moderate social democrats of the center left—only too late did they see what this led to. The democratic left during the Russian Revolution believed it should be allied to Lenin's Bolsheviks to ward off conservative forces and subsequently found out they had committed suicide. The same dynamic is at work even within revolutionary parties. The French Reign of Terror, like Stalin's Russia, Mao's China, the Khmer Rouge regime, and Khomeini's Iran are leading examples. In the fraught circumstances that bring radical utopians to power, the leader who emerges is likely to be ruthless about enforcing his vision, and those who do not totally agree, even if they were once allies and friends, are at great risk.

It may seem natural for those on the right to think that the extreme right is a more reliable ally than the moderate left, or for the moderate left to suppose that the very radical left is a better partner than the moderate right, but when that happens, it becomes more probable that the ultimate winner will be one of the extremes.

CONCLUSION FIVE. Wars, whether with outside powers or internal civil war, invariably enhance the power of the radicals who can claim to be fully committed to the revolution. But if there is no actual war, and little threat of civil war, extremists in power will fabricate such dangers, or provoke them as a way of solidifying their power. The Nazis were masters of such tactics. So was Stalin in the early 1930s when he calumniated his supposedly treacherous domestic enemies, accusing them of foreign alliances, to justify massive purges.

Today putative autocrats in the West foment hysteria about the manageable problem of immigration and terrorism. Even more drastically, Iranian theocrats, Russia's Putin, and Saudi Arabia's would-be totalitarian prince actually engage in low-level war to justify their abuse of power, and they obsessively claim to see immediate threats from foreign sources.

CONCLUSION SIX. We all need to be reminded to pay attention to what political leaders write and say, and never assume that what sounds like extremism is just opportunistic exaggeration. This is another classic error made by centrist reformers and even relatively more moderate revolutionaries. Surely, so the moderates say, smart, educated people can't seriously believe in all those extreme viewpoints, lies, and hysteria. These are just tactics to mobilize their supporters, and once in power those who have peddled such ideas will behave more reasonably. In retrospect it seems almost incomprehensible that moderate leftists failed to grasp in time how utterly ruthless and determined Lenin was. His voluminous writing and policy positions had made that perfectly clear. The same can be said of Hitler. His conservative allies who were not Nazis were hardly liberal, but had they retained power, there would have been no Holocaust. Had they not read *Mein Kampf*? Or did they just not take it seriously? What about Khomeini's writing asserting the need to create a theocratic state where the leading Islamic jurists, led by someone like him, would have the ultimate say in political matters? Did some of his more moderate religious followers forget his position because he was shrewd enough to downplay it when necessary?

What leaders write and say is crucial, but their ideology is also reflected by the symbols they manipulate, and they have to be taken just as seriously. Hitler and Mussolini reveled in the violent symbolism of their brutish street tactics that clearly promised much more nastiness if they took power. The hateful images of their enemies propagated in newspapers, pamphlets, and posters were a warning of what could come. In revolutionary France, Marat's journalism was deliberately violent, so when Robespierre's radical Jacobins took power, it should not have come as a surprise that there would be more bloodshed. Mao was a master of symbolic propaganda, and its violence prefigured his most extreme policies.

What was true then remains the case today. Read carefully what potential political leaders write and say, and if it sounds extreme, do not dismiss their words as mere political posturing. Assume that any approval or encouragement of violence is a prediction of future policies, not just a temporary tactic.

CONCLUSION SEVEN. This book has emphasized the behavior of political elites and how they responded to institutional blockages and crises, and then how they behaved in revolutionary circumstances. But all along there has been another aspect that has come up repeatedly: how ideas were also shaped by cultural and intellectual elites who were not identical to political ones, though the two sets frequently overlapped. Antonio Gramsci's central point in his adaptation of Marxist theory was that the bourgeoisie, or in fact any ruling class, does not rule merely through its economic and political power, but also by imposing cultural values that legitimize its rule.[6] Gramsci wanted to educate the working class in order to create a counterhegemonic culture. We have seen, however, that within the ranks of the very cultural elites who are supposed to defend the system, counterhegemonic philosophies that are precursors of revolutionary change may flourish when necessary reforms are blocked. Enlightenment philosophers in France prepared the way for the revolution by changing ideas well before the late 1780s, and the British and French Enlightenment was part of American elite thinking before the 1770s. Russian opposition among the country's intellectuals to absolutist tsarist rule had been growing for decades before the Revolution of 1917. The rejection of democratic liberal capitalism as too corrupt and compromised began in late nineteenth-century Europe and would eventually play an important role in bringing fascism to power after World War I. Oppositional ferment among Iranian intellectuals should have been a sign to the shah by the early 1970s that all was not well. Antiestablishment ideas do not alone produce revolutions, but they may prepare the ground in delegitimizing existing established political systems and providing theoretical models for new ones, most obviously in revolutionary situations.

What was true in the past remains as true today. The attacks from both the right and the left that today seek to delegitimize liberal capitalist democracy have been at work undermining democracy for decades and now appear to be stronger than ever. It is therefore necessary to pay attention to changing fashions among cultural and intellectual elites to better understand what might happen.[7]

A FINAL, EIGHTH CONCLUSION. If you want a revolution, beware of how it might turn out, because you might one day rue the one that you get. Gradual change, compromise, and flexibility are better ways to adapt to demands for reform. But if there is a revolution, it will take unusual skill, good analysis, and determination by moderate reformers to keep it from turning into tragedy.

These conclusions are so obvious that there should be no need to repeat them or demonstrate their validity. But if the past proves anything, it is that unfortunately those are lessons too often forgotten, or never learned at all. So demonstrating that they are as valid today as ever is necessary, and will be for a long time to come.

NOTES

Chapter 1

1. Isaiah Berlin, one of the best-known liberal philosophers of the twentieth century, commenting on the greatest tragedies of the twentieth century in *Isaiah Berlin: The Power of Ideas*, ed. Henry Hardy (Princeton, NJ: Princeton University Press, 2002), p. 23.

2. Benjamin Constant, *Des Effets de la Terreur*, written in 1797 to denounce the Reign of Terror in the French Revolution. Selected excerpts edited and prefaced by Philippe Reynaud from the 1988 edition (Paris: Flammarion) and available on p. 7 at http://classiques.uqac.ca /classiques/constant_benjamin/effets_de_la_terreur/effets_terreur.html. Constant was one of the foremost French liberals who praised the revolution's original goals but decried the descent into bloody terror. Translation from the French by Chirot.

3. Keith M. Baker, *Condorcet: From Natural Philosophy to Social Mathematics* (Chicago: University of Chicago Press, 1975), and Baker, "Condorcet," in *A Critical Dictionary of the French Revolution*, ed. François Furet and Mona Ozouf, trans. Arthur Goldhammer (1988; Cambridge, MA: Harvard University Press, 1989), pp. 204–212. Emma Rothschild, *Economic Sentiments: Adam Smith, Condorcet, and the Enlightenment* (Cambridge, MA: Harvard University Press, 2001).

4. Patrice Gueniffey, "La Fayette," in Furet and Ozouf, *Critical Dictionary*, pp. 298–312. A recent biography is Laura Auricchio, *The Marquis: Lafayette Reconsidered* (New York: Alfred A. Knopf, 2014).

5. Rothschild, *Economic Sentiments*, pp. 38–39. Ernest Gellner's *Postmodernism, Reason, and Religion* (London: Routledge, 1992) is an elegant defense of the Enlightenment's fundamental skepticism about received and inflexible truths.

6. There will be notes with appropriate references for all of these revolutions in the chapters that follow.

7. Most social science theories of revolution would not accept the idea that fascism, especially Nazi fascism, was revolutionary. Karl Dietrich Bracher ably shows how much the memory of the French Revolution has been used to sustain the false notion that there cannot be a revolutionary far right. "The Janus Face of the French Revolution Today: On Understanding Modern Revolution." In Bracher, *Turning Points in Modern Times: Essays on German and European History*, trans. Thomas Dunlap (1992; Cambridge, MA: Harvard University Press, 1995), pp. 27–44.

Chapter 2

1. On this song see Paul R. Hanson, *Historical Dictionary of the French Revolution* (Lantham MD: Scarecrow Press, 2004), p. 53. Edith Piaf recorded a version of the song: https://www .google.com/search?client=firefox-b-1-d&q=edith+Piaf+%27+ca+ira.

2. Speech by Lenin to an assembly of workers in December 1917, shortly after the October Bolshevik seizure of power. Cited in Nicholas Werth, "A State against Its People: Violence, Repression, and Terror in the Soviet Union." In *The Black Book of Communism: Crimes, Terror, Repression*, ed. Stéphane Courtois, Nicolas Werth, Jean-Louis Panné, Andrzej Packowski, Karel Bartošek, and Jean-Louis Margolin, trans. Jonathan Murphy and Mark Kramer (1997; Cambridge, MA: Harvard University Press, 1999), p. 59.

3. François Furet and Denis Richet, *La Révolution française* (Paris: Hachette, 1973), pp. 28–41. The first edition of this pathbreaking account appeared in 1965 and was read as a sustained attack against the then-current Marxist interpretation of the revolution as a necessary bourgeois uprising against the restrictive remnants of feudalism. See also Jean-Charles Asselain, *Histoire économique de la France du XVIIIe siècle à nos jours*, vol. 1, *De l'Ancien Régime à la première Guerre mondiale* (Paris: Éditions du Seuil, 1984), pp. 9–107. For population figures elsewhere in Europe, see André Armengaud, "Population in Europe 1700–1914," in *The Fontana Economic History of Europe*, ed. Carlo M. Cipolla (London: Collins, 1973), pp. 22–76.

4. Asselain, *Histoire économique*, pp. 25–70; Furet and Richet, *La Révolution française*, pp. 49–67. For more recent scholarship that supports this view of the nature of the crisis facing France, see Peter McPhee, *Liberty or Death: The French Revolution* (New Haven, CT: Yale University Press, 2016), pp. 1–57.

5. This is the main theme of Furet's *Penser la revolution* (Paris: Gallimard, 1978). Marxist historian Eric J. Hobsbawm wrote a nostalgic book that gives an opposite view, that the French Revolution had to take place and was one of the great, good turning points of history because it also inspired more liberation and eventually the later communist revolutions. Hobsbawm, *Echoes of the Marseillaise: Two Centuries Look Back on the French Revolution* (New Brunswick, NJ: Rutgers University Press, 1990). The contrast between these two great historians perfectly illustrates the continuing debates about the French Revolution.

6. This striking contradiction in elite French opinion in the late 1780s played a major role in what subsequently happened. See Furet and Richet, *La Révolution française*, pp. 51–53.

7. Alexis de Tocqueville, *L'Ancien Régime et la Revolution*, 2nd ed. (Paris: Michel Lévy Frères, 1856; the 1st ed. was also published in 1856); see especially pp. 333–345. The classical account, Georges Lefebvre's 1939 work *Quatre-vingt-neuf* [Eighty-nine], translated by R. R. Palmer as *The Coming of the French Revolution*, tells the same story (New York: Vintage Books, 1947), pp. 7–34. More recent scholarship agrees with Lefebvre and Tocqueville. See William Doyle, *The French Revolution: A Very Short Introduction* (Oxford: Oxford University Press, 2001), pp. 19–36.

8. Steve Pincus, *1688: The First Modern Revolution* (New Haven, CT: Yale University Press, 2009). If the English revolutions of 1642 and 1688 are included, the second would undoubtedly be classified with the American as a successful one that avoided many, if not all, of the failures of the ones I am examining. How "modern" 1688 was can be argued, though its outcome clearly

influenced the American Revolution almost nine decades later. Whatever powers Parliament gained, however, what ensued was rule by a tiny elite, not democracy.

9. McPhee, *Liberty or Death*, pp. 58–68. Ran Halévy, "Estates General," in Furet and Ozouf, *Critical Dictionary*, pp. 45–53.

10. Jean-Clément Martin, *Violence et Révolution: Essai sur la naissance d'un mythe national* (Paris: Seuil, 2006), pp. 51–84. Georges Lefebvre, *The Great Fear of 1789*, trans. Joan White (1932; New York: Vintage, 1973). Furet and Richet, *La Révolution française*, pp. 15–98. McPhee, *Liberty or Death*, pp. 58–101, and his chronology, pp. 371–379. See also François Furet, *La Révolution de Turgot à Jules Ferry 1770–1880* (Paris: Hachette, 1988), pp. 54–107, particularly his chronology on pp. 54–55. Furet and Ozouf's edited *Critical Dictionary* is still the best comprehensive, concise source of articles about the leading events, concepts, personalities, ideas, and nineteenth-century interpretations of the French Revolution.

11. Furet and Richet, *La Révolution française*, pp. 99–124, titled their chapter on this part of the revolution "L'année heureuse"—the happy year. See also Timothy Tackett, *The Coming of the Terror in the French Revolution* (Cambridge, MA: Harvard University Press, 2015), pp. 70–95.

12. Gordon S. Wood, *Revolutionary Characters: What Made the Founders Different* (New York: Penguin, 2006).

13. Baker, *Condorcet* and "Condorcet."

14. Tackett, *The Coming of the Terror*, pp. 172–191. See also Albert Soboul's *Les Sans-culottes parisiens en l'an II: Mouvement populaire et gouvernement révolutionaire (1793–1794)* (Paris: Seuil, 1968).

15. In the unofficial but popular anthem of the revolution before "La Marseillaise," "Ça ira, Ça ira," Lafayette is mentioned as a hero. Subsequently, his name was dropped. Hanson, *Historical Dictionary of the French Revolution*, p. 53.

16. Tim McDaniel, *Autocracy, Modernization, and Revolution in Russia and Iran* (Princeton, NJ: Princeton University Press, 1991).

17. An excellent, short account of prerevolutionary Russia can be found in Sheila Fitzpatrick, *The Russian Revolution*, 4th ed. (Oxford: Oxford University Press, 2017), pp. 1–40. A more detailed, classic work is Richard Pipes, *The Russian Revolution*, 2nd ed. (New York: Vintage, 1991), pp. 1–194, as well as Pipes, *Russia under the Old Regime*, 2nd ed. (New York: Penguin Books, 1995). In the latter book Pipes provides a history of how Russia came to be the way it was in the late nineteenth and early twentieth centuries. On Stolypin's effort to save the monarchy while up against a recalcitrant tsar, see Abraham Ascher, *P. A. Stolypin: The Search for Stability in Late Imperial Russia* (Stanford, CA: Stanford University Press, 2001). On the fantastic history of Rasputin, see Douglas Smith, *Rasputin: Faith, Power, and the Twilight of the Romanovs* (New York: Farrar, Straus and Giroux, 2016). Smith tries to be more balanced than most lurid accounts and shows that Rasputin was a complex figure, not just a corrupt, hard-drinking, lecherous lout. On the other hand, the Russian Orthodox Church's recent attempt to make him out to have been a saint is, to say the least, stretching the truth.

18. Heated debates about the origins and causes of World War I continue more than a century later. For a great recent account, see Christopher Clark, *The Sleepwalkers: How Europe Went to War in 1914* (New York: Harper Collins, 2013). On Rasputin's advice and Stolypin's prior

warning, see Sean McMeekin, *The Russian Revolution: A New History* (New York: Basic Books, 2017), pp. 56–59.

19. Cited in Bertram D. Wolfe, *Three Who Made a Revolution* (1948; New York: Cooper Square Press, 2001), p. 558.

20. Another good new source on the period leading up to 1917 is Mark D. Steinberg, *The Russian Revolution 1905–1921* (Oxford: Oxford University Press, 2017), pp. 47–67. See also Jonathan D. Smele, *The "Russian" Civil Wars, 1916–1926: Ten Years That Shook the World* (Oxford: Oxford University Press, 2015), pp. 17–21.

21. T. H. Rigby, *Communist Party Membership in the U.S.S.R., 1917–1967* (Princeton, NJ: Princeton University Press, 1968), pp. 7–8.

22. I am relying on the late British historian Leonard Shapiro. Though his extensive writings on communism were criticized by his more left-wing academic contemporaries, they have held up well. See Leonard Shapiro, *1917: The Russian Revolution and the Origins of Present-Day Communism* (Hounslow, UK: Maurice Temple Smith, 1984), pp. 35–53. More recently, Steinberg, *The Russian Revolution*, pp. 68–91, and Fitzpatrick, *The Russian Revolution*, pp. 41–68, go over the same ground with broadly similar conclusions.

23. While his book presents an overly positive view of Russia's situation immediately before the revolution, Sean McMeekin's recent work does use the now-available evidence of how much support Lenin got from Germany and used to great effect. McMeekin, *The Russian Revolution*, pp. 125–136.

24. Alexander Rabinowitch, *Prelude to Revolution: The Petrograd Bolsheviks and the July 1917 Uprising* (Bloomington: Indiana University Press, 1978).

25. Orlando Figes, *A People's Tragedy: The Russian Revolution 1891–1924* (New York: Penguin, 1997), especially pp. 438–454.

26. As the work of Tim McDaniel and others has shown, what would follow in the October 1917 Revolution was more than just a coup by a tiny group of plotters, as there was very substantial support for the Bolsheviks, though subsequent events would show that had democracy prevailed, it would have been the SRs and perhaps the Mensheviks, not the Bolsheviks, who would have kept power.

27. Shapiro, *1917*, pp. 105–149.

28. The social consequences of this kind of rapid modernization in relatively backward societies are well analyzed in McDaniel, *Autocracy*, especially pp. 70–184.

29. A summary account is Nikki Keddie, *Modern Iran: Roots and Results of Revolution*, updated ed. with a section by Yann Richard (New Haven, CT: Yale University Press, 2006), especially pp. 132–262. For a brief synopsis, see Afshin Matin-Asgari, "The Pahlavi Era," and Maziar Behrooz, "Iran after Revolution," in *The Oxford Handbook of Iranian History*, ed. Touraj Daryaee (New York: Oxford University Press, 2012), chaps. 15 and 16. Charles Kurzman emphasizes the unexpected, unplanned, and chaotic aspects of the revolution in *The Unthinkable Revolution in Iran* (Cambridge, MA: Harvard University Press, 2004). The views of religious Muslims, mostly more liberally inclined ones who supported the revolution but not the radically autocratic and reactionary turn it took, are beautifully explained by Roy Mottahedeh in *The Mantle of the Prophet: Religion and Politics in Iran* (1985; Oxford: Oneworld Publications, 2008). A less well-known but particularly insightful and learned work is Ali Gheissari, *Iranian Intellectuals in the Twentieth Century* (Austin: University of Texas Press, 1998), particularly pp. 74–108, which put

the tremendously influential Ali Shariati in context. There are available YouTube videos of the shah being interviewed in English. Even a few years before his downfall he seemed to have no idea of the reality and strength of the rising opposition, and talked about the love his people had for him, and how great a benevolent father figure he was. For example, see the 1974 interview at www.youtube.com/watch?v=imil1iIpIYA.

30. Ervand Abrahamian, *Khomeinism: Essays on the Islamic Republic* (Berkeley: University of California Press, 1993), especially pp. 17–26.

31. The sequence of events is summarized in Keddie, *Modern Iran*, pp. 240–262. A much more detailed account is in Shaul Bakhash, *The Reign of the Ayatollahs: Iran and the Islamic Revolution* (New York: Basic Books, 1984).

32. Benjamin Carter Hett, *The Death of Democracy: Hitler's Rise to Power and the Downfall of the Weimar Republic* (New York: Henry Holt and Company, 2018), especially chap. 4. Goebbels's promise of a wall is on p. 109.

33. Hett, *The Death of Democracy*. Also, Henry Ashby Turner's *Hitler's Thirty Days to Power* (Reading, MA: Addison Wesley, 1996) shows how massively bad judgment by conservatives put Hitler in power. There is, as with other cases presented here, an enormous literature on what happened. Volker Ulrich's *Hitler: Ascent 1889–1939*, trans. Jefferson S. Chase (2013; New York: Alfred A. Knopf, 2016) emphasizes that many Germans failed to recognize in time that Hitler was a clever, skillful politician whose lies had created a very enthusiastic following. Ian Kershaw's two volumes, *Hitler: 1889–1963 Hubris* and *Hitler: 1936–1945 Nemesis* (New York: W. W. Norton, 1999 and 2000), remain definitive. Jeffrey Herf's *Reactionary Modernism: Technology, Culture, and Politics in Weimar and the Third Reich* (Cambridge: Cambridge University Press, 1984) is strong on the intellectual background of reactionary, anti-Enlightenment ideology and culture as a response to unsettling modernization.

34. Donald Sassoon's *Mussolini and the Rise of Fascism* (London: Harper Collins, 2007) convincingly shows that conservatives looking for some way of enlisting mass support decided that Mussolini's fascists could do it for them even though his movement was still relatively small. More deeply analytical, Zeev Sternhell, with Mario Sznajder and Maia Asheri, *The Birth of Fascist Ideology*, trans. David Maisel (1989; Princeton, NJ: Princeton University Press, 1994), shows that it was not just Mussolini but a well-rooted intellectual tradition that supported not only Italian but many other versions of fascism. On Mussolini and the larger context of his rise, see R.J.B. Bosworth, *Mussolini* (London: Bloomsbury Academic, 2010).

Chapter 3

1. Thomas Carlyle, *The French Revolution*, Modern Library (New York: Random House, 1954), p. 669. Carlyle's classic was first published in 1837.

2. Mao Tse-tung, *Quotations from Chairman Mao-Tse-tung* (Peking: Foreign Language Press, 1966), p. 60. This first-edition English translation of Mao's famous "Little Red Book" was printed at the beginning of the Cultural Revolution. It still transcribed Chinese words according to the old Wade-Giles system, before Pinyin romanization was adopted.

3. Maya Jasanoff, *Liberty's Exiles: American Loyalists in the Revolutionary World* (New York: Knopf, 2011). This new interpretation shows that these exiles contributed significantly to reforming the British Empire into something more viable and responsive to change.

4. Michel Biard and Hervé Leuwers, *Danton: Le Mythe et l'histoire* (Paris: Armand Colin, 2016), second and third pages of the introduction, pp. 9–11 of the electronic edition. Electronic pagination is unreliable as it depends on how the text is viewed.

5. Furet, "Vendée," in Furet and Ozouf, *Critical Dictionary*, pp. 165–176. There were *bocages* (hedgerows of raised earth overlaid with bushes and trees between fields) covering the Vendée and much of the western region, into Brittany and Normandy. They demarcated fields and provided firewood but seriously impeded the revolution's armies by making counterrevolutionary guerrilla warfare easier. More recently, from June to early August of 1944, the *bocages* made the German resistance to Allied troops in Normandy particularly difficult to overcome. Among other now-classic attempts to explain the rebellion, see Charles Tilly, *The Vendée* (Cambridge, MA: Harvard University Press, 1964); Claude Petitfrère, *La Vendée et les Vendéens* (Paris: Gallimard-Juliard, 1981); and, most recently, the work of the prolific French historian Jean-Clément Martin, *La Guerre de Vendée, 1793–1800* (Paris: Point-Seuil, 2014). The estimate of the number of deaths is from Tackett, *The Coming of the Terror*, chap. 12, the paragraph ending with n40.

6. W. D. Edmonds, *Jacobinism and the Revolt of Lyon 1789–1793* (Oxford: Oxford University Press, 1990). Executions in Lyon continued well into 1794, months after the city had been subdued. On Fouché, see the popular classic 1929 biography by the Austrian author Stefan Zweig, *Joseph Fouché: Portrait of a Politician*, trans. Eden and Cedar Paul (New York: Viking, 1930). A more definitive, scholarly work is Jean Tulard, *Joseph Fouché* (Paris: Fayard, 1998).

7. Philippe Delorme, *Louis XVII, la vérité: Sa mort au Temple confirmée par la science* (Paris: Pygmalion, 2000). Louis XVII's uncle Louis XVIII had records about what happened destroyed when he came to power after Napoleon's fall, thus giving rise to legends about the boy's possible survival.

8. Ozouf, "Girondins," in Furet and Ozouf, *Critical Dictionary*, pp. 351–362.

9. François-Alphonse Aulard, *Les Grands Orateurs de la Révolution. Mirabeau, Vergniaud, Danton, Robespierre* (Paris: F. Rieder, 1914). Chap. 7 is on Danton, whom Aulard defends against the charges of corruption and opposition to the revolution, and chap. 4 on Robespierre, who is portrayed as a brilliant orator but a narrow, unsympathetic combination of fanatic and opportunist, jealous, power hungry, and a murderer. This reprises the earlier, more substantial Aulard work, *Danton* (Paris: Picard-Bernheim, 1887) and is also a summary of the extensive work on revolutionary orators published earlier by Aulard. Aulard was the first appointee to the chair for the study of the French Revolution at the University of Paris, a Third Republic innovation meant to legitimize the liberal side of the revolution.

10. Stephen F. Cohen turned Bukharin into a moderate hero in *Bukharin and the Bolshevik Revolution: A Political Biography, 1888–1938*, 2nd ed. (New York: Oxford University Press, 1980). In some sense he truly was more moderate than Stalin for well-thought-out tactical reasons, but he was nevertheless a committed Bolshevik revolutionary willing to use force to further the revolution's goals. A moving account of what happened to Bukharin is Roy A. Medvedev, *Bukharin: The Last Years*, trans. A.D.P Briggs (New York: W. W. Norton, 1980). See also Stephen F. Cohen, *Soviet Fates and the Lost Alternatives: From Stalinism to the New Cold War* (New York: Columbia University Press, 2009).

11. Crane Brinton's classic analysis of revolutions and their inevitable "Thermidorian" re-

action after the reign of the extremists is still worth reading. His *Anatomy of Revolution*, 3rd rev. ed. (New York: Prentice Hall, 1965) was originally published in 1938. See especially chap. 8, pp. 205–236. Furet and Richet, *La Révolution française*, pp. 125–254. McPhee, *Liberty or Death*, pp. 142–273. Furet, *La Révolution de Turgot à Jules Ferry*, pp. 110–157, particularly the chronology on pp. 110–111. Tackett, *The Coming of the Terror*, chap. 4 through the conclusion, covers this period. So does Martin, *Violence et Révolution*, pp. 85–236.

12. Albert Mathiez, *The French Revolution*, trans. Catherine Alison Phillips (1922; New York: Alfred A. Knopf, 1928). The quote is from p. 509. On the whole Eric J. Hobsbawm agrees with Mathiez. See his classic 1962 book, *The Age of Revolution 1789–1848* (New York: Mentor paperback, 1964), pp. 91–95. The 1983 film *Danton* directed by the famed Polish director Andrzej Wajda portrays Robespierre as an early version of Lenin. It makes Danton out to be a more benign liberal, also mostly a myth.

13. Biard and Leuwers, *Danton*. See in particular chap. 10 by Leuwers, "Danton et Robespierre. Le duel réinventé." Also chap. 14 by Annie Duprat and Pascal Dupuy, "Danton l'insaisissable. Images et mémoires." The Abbé Sieyès, a former priest, had become prominent in 1789 with a widely read pamphlet demanding more power for the Third Estate, but he regained great influence only during the post-Thermidor Directory. Keith M. Baker, "Sieyès," in Furet and Ozouf, *Critical Dictionary*, pp. 313–323. See also note 22 and the accompanying text below. On the occasion of the two hundredth anniversary of the revolution, in 1989, Robespierre, Danton, and La Fayette were by far the most recognized names from that period in France, but the latter two were generally viewed far more favorably.

14. Though there are many studies of the Cheka, a particularly good account of its many activities is available in Robert Service's *Spies and Commissars: The Early Years of the Russian Revolution* (Philadelphia: PublicAffairs, 2012).

15. The complexities of this series of wars would require a whole book to explain all of what happened. Very many have been written, including memoirs by participants. An excellent account that was able to take advantage of recently available documents as well as the ample older historiography is Smele, *The "Russian" Civil Wars*. Smele put "Russian" in quotation marks because he shows that much fighting was not specifically Russian but involved many ethnic groups and regions that did not all remain within Russia. His starting point is 1916 because revolts broke out against the Russian state in Central Asia in that year. Very useful, also, is Evan Mawdsley, *The Russian Civil War* (Boston: Allen & Unwin, 1987). Mawdsley's terminology and dating are the more common, but he did not yet have access to the archives opened for a while after the collapse of the USSR.

16. Paul Avrich, *Kronstadt 1921* (Princeton, NJ: Princeton University Press, 1970).

17. Smele, *The "Russian" Civil Wars*, pp. 159–164. There are vivid eyewitness descriptions in Isaac Babel's "Red Cavalry Stories." *The Complete Works of Isaac Babel*, ed. Nathalie Babel, trans. Peter Constantine (New York: W. W. Norton, 2002). The stories are scattered among pp. 197–375. Babel's personal diary contained even more vivid, horrible details. For the role of Jews under Russian communism, see Yuri Slezkine, *The Jewish Century* (Princeton, NJ: Princeton University Press, 2004), especially chap. 3, "Babel's First Love: The Jews and the Russian Revolution," pp. 105–203.

18. World War I deaths are from the Centre Robert Schuman, "Reperes": http://www.centre

-robert-schuman.org/userfiles/files/REPERES%20-%20module%201-1-1%20-%20 explanatory%20notes%20-%20World%20War%20I%20casualties%20-%20EN.pdf. Civil war estimates are from Smele, *The "Russian" Civil Wars*, p. 3 and p. 256n8.

19. Smele, *The "Russian" Civil Wars*, pp. 173–188. On the peasant question and the way Lenin's insistence on interpreting everything through class warfare created a need to find an exploiting "kulak" or rich peasant class where none existed, see Teodor Shanin, *The Awkward Class: Political Sociology of Peasantry in a Developing Society; Russia 1910–1925* (Oxford: Clarendon Press, 1972).

20. Rigby, *Communist Party Membership*, pp. 7–8, 52. Steinberg, *The Russian Revolution*, pp. 101–105.

21. See the essays edited by Sheila Fitzpatrick, Alexander Rabinowitch, and Richard Stites, *Russia in the Era of NEP* (Bloomington: Indiana University Press, 1991).

22. McPhee, *Liberty or Death*, pp. 274–341. Furet and Richet, *La Révolution française*, pp. 257–513. Jacques-Olivier Boudon, *Histoire du Consulat et de l'Empire* (Paris: Perrin, 2000), pp. 13–64. Furet, *La Révolution de Turgot à Jules Ferry*, pp. 158–213, with the chronology on pp. 158–159. Jean Tulard, *Napoleon: The Myth of the Saviour*, trans. Teresa Waugh (1977; London: Methuen & Co., 1985), pp. 1–18. Sieyès continued to play an important supporting role in what followed. On Sieyès's long career and the importance of his political thought, see William H. Sewell, Jr., *A Rhetoric of Bourgeois Revolution: The Abbé Sieyès and What Is the Third Estate?* (Durham NC: Duke University Press, 1964). See also note 13 to this chapter and note 5 to chap. 5 below and the accompanying text. His 1789 pamphlet on the Third Estate became prominent again in the mid-twentieth century. Talleyrand went on to serve as Napoleon's foreign minister, then betrayed him in 1814, and played a key role at the Congress of Vienna that reshaped Europe for decades to come. On Talleyrand's extraordinary life, see David Lawday, *Napoleon's Master: Prince Talleyrand* (New York: St. Martin's Press, 2007). He had also been the main mastermind of the Egyptian adventure. See Georges Lacour-Gayet, *Talleyrand* (1947; Paris: Éditions Payot, 1990), pp. 315–341. But the notion that anyone was ever Napoleon's "master" seems far-fetched.

23. Karl Marx, *The Eighteenth Brumaire of Louis Bonaparte*. This was originally published in 1852 and has been reprinted many times. David McLellan, *Karl Marx: Selected Writings* (Oxford: Oxford University Press, 1977), pp. 300–337.

24. Laurent Dubois, *Avengers of the New World: The Story of the Haitian Revolution* (Cambridge, MA: Harvard University Press, 2004), p. 284 on the reinstitution of slavery, and the whole book for the whole story. See also the more recent Jeremy Popkin, *You Are All Free: The Haitian Revolution and the Abolition of Slavery* (New York: Cambridge University Press, 2010), on the widespread fear and loathing the Haitian Revolution inspired in European and American slave owners, and the long-term consequences.

25. Steven Englund, *Napoleon: A Political Life* (Cambridge, MA: Harvard University Press, 2004), p. 189.

26. The detailed, superbly researched book by Boudon, *Histoire du Consulat et de l'Empire*, would seem to be definitive, but with Napoleon there will always be new books and interpretations. The older but also authoritative French biography by Tulard, *Napoléon*, remains worthwhile. Even earlier was Georges Lefebvre's two-volume work, *Napoléon*, that covers the period

from the 18th of Brumaire to the end (Paris: Presses universitaires de France, 1935–1936). This biography has remained in print in new French and English editions. More recently there is Englund, *Napoleon*. See also Patrice Gueniffey, *Bonaparte 1769–1802* (Paris: Gallimard, 2013). It is only the first volume of a more complete forthcoming biography but is meant to be a definitive study. There is a Harvard University Press English translation, published in 2015. David A. Bell's short but excellent synthesis of both the reality and the legend of Napoleon is in his *Napoleon: A Concise Biography* (Oxford: Oxford University Press, 2015). Sudhir Hazareesingh, *The Legend of Napoleon* (London: Granta, 2004), is more about the birth of the myths that have enraptured France and the world since his fall. See also, once more, Furet, *La Révolution de Turgot à Jules Ferry*, pp. 214–267, with the chronology on pp. 214–215.

27. On the incredible career of Bernadotte, who went from being a commoner to marshal of France to king of Sweden and founder of the Swedish royal family, see Franck Favier, *Bernadotte, un maréchal d'Empire sur le trône de Suède* (Paris: Ellipse, 2010). Bernadotte cleverly joined the allies against his former friend and relative Napoleon (by marriage), and so was accepted by the rest of Europe.

28. Lionel Jospin (a former socialist French prime minister), *Le mal napoléonien* (Paris: Seuil, 2014), is hostile to Napoleon. Dominique de Villepin (a former conservative French prime minister), *Le soleil noir de la puissance 1796–1807* (Paris: Perrin, 2009) and *Les Cent-Jours, ou, L'esprit de sacrifice* (Paris: Perrin 2001), is favorable. For Villepin Napoleon is still France's greatest hero. The British critic Stephen Clarke wrote: "Two centuries on, the French are still in denial about Waterloo. Victor Hugo, the historian Jules Michelet, and now Villepin have claimed that at Waterloo Napoleon and his heroic imperial guard scored a 'moral victory.' " Clarke then quotes Napoleon himself, who supposedly said, "History is a series of lies on which we all agree." Stephen Clarke, "Facing Their Waterloo: The French Would Still Prefer to Think of Napoleon's Last Defeat as a Moral Victory," *Spectator*, June 13, 2015, p. 24. See the fascinating juxtaposition of France's two most famous leaders after 1789 in Patrice Gueniffey, *Napoléon et de Gaulle: Deux héros français* (Paris: Perrin, 2017).

29. The most definitive recent account of Stalin's rise to power is in Stephen Kotkin's masterful, *Stalin: Paradoxes of Power, 1878–1928* (New York: Penguin, 2015). Particularly important for understanding this stage of Stalin's career is chap. 10, "Dictator." James Harris has made the point that by reassuring many thousands of lesser, local party officials who might be less competent and even corrupt, Stalin was able to keep them loyal as he gradually moved to strengthen the party apparatus and his own control. See his "Stalin as General Secretary: The Appointment Process and the Nature of Stalin's Power," in *Stalin: A New History*, ed. Sarah Davies and James Harris (Cambridge: Cambridge University Press, 2005), pp. 63–82.

30. Robert Tucker, *Stalin as Revolutionary 1879–1929* (New York: W. W. Norton, 1974), p. 393. Cohen, *Bukharin*, pp. 147–148.

31. Though somewhat dated, Isaac Deutscher's monumental, admiring, three-volume biography of Trotsky remains the best way to get to the heart of the man. The volumes were published from 1954 to 1963 when it still seemed Soviet communism had a chance to reform itself. By the time they were republished in 2003, that illusion had passed and Trotsky was less well remembered. *The Prophet Armed: Trotsky 1879–1921*; *The Prophet Unarmed: Trotsky 1921–29*; *The Prophet Outcast: Trotsky 1929–40* (New York: Verso, 2003). Volume 2 is the most

relevant here. The bulk of Trotsky's most famous works—those that won him many devoted supporters who believed in communism but thought that Stalin had betrayed the ideal—were, however, written while he was an "outcast." A reader without the patience to read through more than a thousand pages can get a good idea of what they contain in Neal Ascherson, "Victory in Defeat," *London Review of Books* 26, no. 23 (December 2, 2004), https://www.lrb .co.uk/v26/n23/neal-ascherson/victory-in-defeat. There is much material about the Trotsky-Stalin rivalry and all the maneuvering that went on in Kotkin, *Stalin: Paradoxes of Power*, chap. 11, "Remove Stalin."

32. Stephen Kotkin's second Stalin volume, *Stalin: Waiting for Hitler 1929–1941* (New York: Penguin, 2017), especially pp. 411–415. Kotkin in this volume also explains the purges of the 1930s, about which there will be more below. See also Simon Sebag Montefiore, *Stalin: The Court of the Red Tsar* (New York: Vintage / Random House, 2005), pp. 58–61, 219–244. Also Walter Laqueur, *Stalin: The Glasnost Revelations* (New York: Scribner, 1990), p. 91.

33. Benjamin Carter Hett, *Burning the Reichstag: An Investigation into the Third Reich's Enduring Mystery* (New York: Oxford University Press, 2014). Also Hett, *The Death of Democracy*, chap. 7.

34. Bracher mentions the "Night of the Long Knives" as a possible "second" revolution that allowed Hitler to pass laws and decrees opening the way to more terror and radical change. "The Janus Face of the French Revolution Today," p. 34. Hett, *The Death of Democracy*, chap. 8.

35. Kerry Brown, *Friends and Enemies: The Past, Present and Future of the Communist Party of China* (London: Anthem Press, 2009). See pp. 25–54, which discuss purges before the final communist victory in 1949 that in a sense paved the way for subsequent purges. On more recent purges, see Brown's *CEO, China: The Rise of Xi Jinping* (London: I. B. Taurus, 2016).

36. The entire early part of the revolution is well summarized in chap. 3 of Michael Axworthy, *Revolutionary Iran: A History of the Islamic Republic* (New York: Oxford University Press, 2013).

37. America's leading foreign-policy institutions, most critically the CIA and State Department, had badly misunderstood Iran for a long time. This contributed to the mishandling of the situation from 1978 to 1980. See Gary Sick's recounting of what happened in his *All Fall Down: America's Tragic Encounter with Iran* (New York: Random House, 1986).

38. Axworthy, *Revolutionary Iran*, chaps. 4 and 5.

39. Ibid., chap. 7.

Chapter 4

1. Hitler's last testament, April 29, 1945, dictated the day before his suicide in his Berlin bunker, https://www.yadvashem.org/docs/hitler-testament.html.

2. Eric Hobsbawm, *The Age of Extremes: A History of the World, 1914–1991* (New York: Vintage / Random House, 1996), pp. 389–390.

3. I explored the theme of ideological inflexibility in Chirot, *Modern Tyrants: The Power and Prevalence of Evil in Our Age*, 2nd ed. (Princeton, NJ: Princeton University Press, 1994), chap. 3.

4. Alan Knight, *The Mexican Revolution: A Very Short Introduction* (Oxford: Oxford University Press, 2016), summarizes the very complicated events, causes, and outcomes of the revolu-

tion. This is a much-updated account that supplements his earlier, more detailed *The Mexican Revolution* (Cambridge: Cambridge University Press, 1986).

5. On Villa, the major study is Friedrich Katz's massive *The Life and Times of Pancho Villa* (Stanford, CA: Stanford University Press, 1998). Katz affirms that the government was certainly involved in what has long been seen as a murky plot to murder Villa, and the United States may have encouraged it too, as there was fear of another Villa uprising. See Katz, pp. 761–782. The now-classic study of Zapata by John Womack, *Zapata and the Mexican Revolution* (New York: Alfred A. Knopf, 1969), perhaps overromanticizes Zapata, though not as much as the exciting, if more or less historically accurate, 1952 film starring Marlon Brando, *Viva Zapata!*. More recent and balanced is Paul Hart's *Emiliano Zapata: Mexico's Social Revolutionary* (New York: Oxford University Press, 2018). On the power and influence of Zapata's mythologized legacy, see Samuel Brunk, *The Posthumous Career of Emiliano Zapata: Myth, Memory, and Mexico's Twentieth Century* (Austin: University of Texas Press, 2008).

6. Jürgen Buchenau, *The Last Caudillo: Álvaro Obregón and the Mexican Revolution* (Malden: Wiley-Blackwell, 2011). The early alliance with COM is discussed on pp. 65–66.

7. Jean Meyer, *The Cristero Rebellion: The Mexican People between Church and State, 1926–1929* (Cambridge: Cambridge University Press, 1976), p. 207.

8. Buchenau, *The Last Caudillo*, pp. 152–163.

9. The best account is Meyer, *The Cristero Rebellion*. This book makes it clear that the faith of ordinary peasants and some in the working class played a crucial role in provoking this revolt against the state's secularization policies. Meyer is clearly sympathetic to the genuine Catholic faith of the lower class and village priests, and perhaps overestimates the centralizing power of the Mexican state, but his combination of archival research and interviews with surviving participants is convincing.

10. Jürgen Buchenau's *Plutarco Elías Calles and the Mexican Revolution* (Lanham, MD: Rowman & Littlefield, 2007), especially pp. 81–172.

11. Knight's 2016 *Mexican Revolution* neatly summarizes the last part of the revolution and the subsequent institutionalization of PRI rule, pp. 104–116. Nora Hamilton has argued that unless capitalism is overturned—and particularly when foreign interests are so powerful, as was the case in the American-Mexican relationship—a state cannot thoroughly push through radical reform. Even under Cárdenas there were strict limits to what the revolution could achieve. *The Limits of State Autonomy: Post-Revolutionary Mexico* (Princeton, NJ: Princeton University Press, 1982). Of course if only something like Fidel Castro's Cuba is the model for what a proper revolution should be, then Mexico's was an aborted failure.

12. This is well summarized in Katz, *The Life and Times of Pancho Villa*, pp. 795–818.

13. See Knight's classic article "The Mexican Revolution: Bourgeois? Nationalist? Or Just a 'Great Rebellion'?," *Bulletin of Latin American Research* 4, no. 2 (1986): 1–37. On why interpretations of the revolution have varied so much and been contentious, see his "The Myth of the Mexican Revolution," *Past and Present*, no. 209 (November 2010): 223–273.

14. Leonard Folgarait, *Mural Painting and Social Revolution in Mexico, 1920–1940* (New York: Cambridge University Press, 1998).

15. Adolf Hitler, *Mein Kampf*, trans. Ralph Mannheim (1925; Boston: Houghton Mifflin, 1971). The quotes are, respectively, on pp. 296, 139–140, and 327.

16. Herbert F. Ziegler, *Nazi Germany's New Aristocracy: The SS Leadership, 1925–1939* (Princeton, NJ: Princeton University Press, 1989). This book has a detailed account of the social background and educational attainment of SS leaders. Many were well-educated professionals, particularly among those who joined after the Nazis came to power, but there were others from more humble origins too.

17. This is hardly the place to recount the story of World War II. Probably the best single volume that tells it, including the Pacific War, is the monumental work of Gerhard L. Weinberg, *A World at Arms: A Global History of World War II* (Cambridge: Cambridge University Press, 1994).

18. On the Nazi economy, see Adam Tooze, *The Wages of Destruction: The Making and Breaking of the Nazi Economy* (New York: Penguin, 2008), especially chaps. 1–9, addressing the period before the start of the war. On the Gestapo, Robert Gellately, *The Gestapo and German Society: Enforcing Racial Policy 1933–1945* (New York: Oxford University Press, 1992). On the attempt to reshape society, Detlev J. K. Peukert, *Inside Nazi Germany: Conformity, Opposition, and Racism in Everyday Life*, trans. Richard Deveson (1982; New Haven, CT: Yale University Press, 1987). Peukert shows that there was a good bit of passive resistance, but it could hardly do much to change the political situation. Karl Dietrich Bracher, "Resistance in 'Right Dictatorships,'" in Bracher, *Turning Points*, pp. 154–158, shows that there was in fact very little effective resistance, and it got weaker as the Nazi regime became more entrenched.

19. Scott L. Montgomery and Daniel Chirot, *The Shape of the New: Four Big Ideas and How They Made the Modern World* (Princeton, NJ: Princeton University Press, 2015), chap. 5.

20. Timothy Snyder, *Bloodlands: Europe between Hitler and Stalin* (New York: Basic Books, 2010), pp. 155–276. On the killing of Jews, among many other very fine works there are Raul Hilberg, *Perpetrators Victims Bystanders: The Jewish Catastrophe 1933–1945* (New York: Harper-Collins, 1992), and Saul Friedländer, *Nazi Germany and the Jews 1939–1945* (New York: Harper-Collins, 2007). Snyder provides some approximation of numbers of deaths on p. 155. Ian Kershaw, *The End: The Defiance and Destruction of Hitler's Germany, 1944–1945* (New York: Penguin, 2011), has numbers on pp. 376 and 379. Careful historians like Snyder and Kershaw are generally cautious about assigning precise numbers as there is no way of knowing exactly. Though it is often unwise to use Wikipedia as a source, its estimate of the number of World War II deaths in the article "World War II Casualties" is quite careful and is as good as any available: https://en.wikipedia.org/wiki/World_War_II_casualties.

21. Karel C. Berkhoff, *Harvest of Despair: Life and Death in Ukraine under Nazi Rule* (Cambridge, MA: Harvard University Press, 2004).

22. Julian Jackson, *France: The Dark Years 1940–1944* (Oxford: Oxford University Press, 2001). Hitler, *Mein Kampf*, pp. 616–621.

23. Kershaw, *The End*, pp. 154–155 and 348–377. This superb book explains in fascinating detail how it was that the war lasted so long.

24. Montgomery and Chirot, *The Shape of the New*, pp. 81–110.

25. Kotkin, *Stalin*, 2:9–22. R. W. Davies, "Stalin as Economic Policy-Maker: Soviet Agriculture, 1931–1936," in Davies and Harris, *Stalin*, pp. 121–124.

26. Kotkin, *Stalin*, 2:31–50.

27. Ibid., 2:122–130. Much of Robert Conquest's work about the Stalinist purges and forced

famines was decried by more leftist analysts, but the vast trove of new archives opened after the fall of the Soviet Union in 1991 and research since then have shown that by and large he was right. See his book *The Harvest of Sorrow: Soviet Collectivization and the Terror Famine* (New York: Oxford University Press, 1986). See also Snyder, *Bloodlands*, pp. 21–58. Snyder here, as elsewhere in his book, is cautious about overestimating the number of deaths, but there were undoubtedly many millions. Probably the most careful estimate of seven to eight million is in Nicholas Werth, "Forced Collectivization and Dekulakization," in Courtois et al., *The Black Book of Communism*, pp. 141–202 and some of the pictures that follow p. 202. For personal stories of what collectivization did to private lives, nothing is better than Orlando Figes, *The Whisperers: Private Life in Stalin's Russia* (New York: Metropolitan Books, 2007), chaps. 2 and 3. Figes covers the entire Soviet period and its aftermath, but concentrates on Stalin's rule from 1925 to 1953.

28. R. W. Davies, "Stalin as Economic Policy-Maker," p. 139.

29. Leon Trotsky, *The Revolution Betrayed: What Is the Soviet Union and Where Is It Going?* (New York: Doubleday, 1937), p. 273. Trotsky, who hardly hesitated to be brutal, accused Stalin of using "petty bourgeois" methods. "Petty bourgeois" and "Bonapartist" were two of the greatest insults Marxist-Leninists used to denigrate their ideological enemies, though for Stalin "Trotskyites" were even more dangerous.

30. Amy Knight, in *Who Killed Kirov? The Kremlin's Greatest Mystery* (New York: Hill & Wang, 1999), makes a strong case for blaming Stalin. Matthew E. Lenoe, *The Kirov Murder and Soviet History* (New Haven, CT: Yale University Press, 2010), disagrees and concludes it was the work of a lone discontent despite the volume of conflicting evidence that makes it impossible to be entirely certain. J. Arch Getty, *Origins of the Great Purges: The Soviet Communist Party Reconsidered, 1933–1938* (Cambridge: Cambridge University Press, 1985), does not believe in Stalin's guilt. Kotkin, in *Stalin*, 2:197–237, supports the notion that the Kirov murder was the origin of later purges, though it took time for Stalin to turn this into such large-scale killing. But while he shows that there were many reasons to suspect Stalin and the clearly rigged investigation that followed the murder, Kotkin avoids directly implicating him.

31. Kotkin, *Stalin*, 2:305. Werth, in Courtois et al., *The Black Book of Communism*, pp. 184–215, estimates about a million deaths from the purges, and close to two million prisoners present in the Gulag by January 1940. These are necessarily low estimates because they do not count those who died without ever being registered, and also because so many different categories of people were arrested in varying circumstances.

32. Snyder, *Bloodlands*, pp. 89–109, details the fate of the Poles. Kotkin, *Stalin*, 2:434–460. On the Korean deportation in 1937, see the 2007 documentary film by Y. David Chung, Matt Dibble, and Meredith Jung-en Woo, *Koryo Saram: The Unreliable People*. For the later cases of the Chechen-Ingush and Crimean Tatars, Norman Naimark, *Fires of Hatred: Ethnic Cleansing in Twentieth-Century Europe* (Cambridge, MA: Harvard University Press, 2001), pp. 85–107. Also, more generally on Stalin's crimes, Norman Naimark, *Stalin's Genocides* (Princeton, NJ: Princeton University Press, 2010).

33. See the interesting Khrushchev memoirs edited and translated by his son Sergei Khrushchev, *Memoirs of Nikita Khrushchev*, vol. 2, *Reformer 1945–1964* (1999; University Park: Pennsylvania State University Press, 2006), pp. 201–221.

34. Some major references include Jonathan Spence's *The Search for Modern China* (New

York: W. W. Norton, 1990), pp. 216–540, and his short *Mao Zedong: A Life* (New York: Penguin, 1999), pp. 1–119. On the key May 4th movement that radicalized young Chinese intellectuals, Vera Schwartz, *The Chinese Enlightenment: Intellectuals and the Legacy of the May Fourth Movement of 1919* (Berkeley: University of California Press, 1986). On Germany as a model, William C. Kirby, *Germany and Republican China* (Stanford, CA: Stanford University Press, 1984). More recently, Odd Arne Westad, *Decisive Encounters: The Chinese Civil War, 1946–1950* (Stanford, CA: Stanford University Press, 2003), and Sun Shuyun, *The Long March: The True History of China's Founding Myth* (New York: Anchor Books, 2008). Both these books make it clear how mythologized the civil war and Long March have been. Jay Taylor, in *The Generalissimo: Chiang Kai-shek and the Struggle for Modern China* (Cambridge, MA: Harvard University Press, 2009), shows that Chiang was indeed a committed modernizer and a revolutionary of sorts, not just an inept, corrupt dictator. In that sense the best-selling book by Barbara Tuchman, *Stillwell and the American Experience in China: 1911–1945* (New York: Macmillan, 1970), is misleading.

35. Rudolph J. Rummel, *China's Bloody Century: Genocide and Mass Murder since 1900* (1991; New York: Routledge, 2017), pp. 1–203. Rummel's sources were in European languages. For obvious reasons it is impossible to verify his numbers with Chinese sources, and his estimates are unrealistically precise. On the other hand, he was a careful compiler of data and his general conclusions are entirely reasonable, even conservative.

36. Jean-Louis Margolin, "China: A Long March into Night," in Courtois et al., *The Black Book of Communism*, pp. 476–480.

37. Nicholas Lardy, *Agriculture in China's Modern Economic Development* (New York: Cambridge University Press, 1983). Margolin, "China," pp. 480–487. The quote is cited in Lynn T. White III, *The Politics of Chaos: The Organizational Causes of Violence in China's Cultural Revolution* (Princeton, NJ: Princeton University Press, 1989), p. 222. On the Korean War, Bruce Cummings, *Korea's Place in the Sun: A Modern History* (New York: W. W. Norton, 1997), pp. 237–298.

38. Spence, *The Search for Modern China*, pp. 569–573.

39. Lorenz M. Lüthi, *The Sino-Soviet Split: Cold War in the Communist World* (Princeton, NJ: Princeton University Press, 2008), especially pp. 46–113.

40. David Brandenberger, "Stalin as Symbol: A Case Study of the Personality Cult and Its Construction," in Davies and Harris, *Stalin*, pp. 249–270. Spence, *Mao Zedong*, pp. 132–134. On Ho Chi Minh see below, particularly note 56 and the accompanying text.

41. Cited in Lowell Dittmer, *China's Continuous Revolution: The Post-Liberation Epoch 1949–1981* (Berkeley: University of California Press, 1987), p. 32.

42. Roderick MacFarquhar, *The Origins of the Cultural Revolution*, vol. 2, *The Great Leap Forward 1958–1960* (New York: Columbia University Press, 1983), p. 103.

43. Harrison E. Salisbury, *The New Emperors: China in the Era of Mao and Deng* (Boston: Little, Brown, 1992), pp. 218–219.

44. The highest estimate is in Frank Dikötter's *Mao's Great Famine: The History of China's Most Devastating Catastrophe, 1958–1962* (London: Bloomsbury, 2010). A long review article by Felix Wemheuer questions the numbers and the way in which Dikötter sometimes generalized from relatively few examples, in "Sites of Horror: Mao's Great Famine," *China Journal* 66 (July 2011): 155–164. Wemheuer also criticizes the book for not mentioning earlier Chinese famines,

including ones for which the Nationalists could be blamed. Dikötter rebuts the criticism on pp. 162–164 by referring to the many provincial archives he was able to consult. Citing only official Chinese sources, Nicholas Lardy earlier estimated there were sixteen to twenty-eight million deaths, in *Agriculture in China's Modern Economic Development*, pp. 41–43, 150–152. Also, Spence, *Mao Zedong*, p. 149. Judith Shapiro's *Mao's War against Nature* (Cambridge: Cambridge University Press, 2001), pp. 66–93, adds to our understanding of what happened by showing that this episode caused disastrous environmental destruction. Mao, quite typically for Marxist leaders, believed that nature could be overcome, no matter what the environmental cost.

45. Spence, *Mao Zedong*, pp. 144–148.

46. Margolin, "China," pp. 513–538. The quote is on p. 529. For more comprehensive references about the Cultural Revolution, see note 47 below. On the Red Guards, there is Andrew Walder, *Fractured Rebellion: The Beijing Red Guard Movement* (Cambridge, MA: Harvard University Press, 2012). Walder shows that it is impossible to assign specific class or background characteristics to various factions that fought pitched battles against each other.

47. The best sources on the Cultural Revolution remain the three volumes by Roderick MacFarquhar, *The Origins of the Cultural Revolution* (New York: Columbia University Press, 1974–1997), and a significantly updated summary (but still massive) volume by MacFarquhar and Michael Schoenhals, *Mao's Last Revolution* (Cambridge, MA: Harvard University Press, 2006). Particularly instructive on intraparty struggles and the purging of much of the old elite are pp. 253–336 of *Mao's Last Revolution*. This also includes a discussion of the end of Liu Shaoqi and Lin Biao. There are now a vast number of personal recollections about the catastrophic disruption, the tragedies, the violence, and the sheer madness of what Mao set off. A good example is Ma Bo, *Blood Red Sunset: A Memoir of the Chinese Cultural Revolution*, trans. Howard Goldblatt (New York: Penguin, 1996). In a brief, recent article, Roderick MacFarquhar notes that in contemporary China the Cultural Revolution has become an almost forbidden, unacknowledged historical episode, and that we should not be so sure that it can never again happen. See his "The Once and Future Tragedy of the Cultural Revolution," *China Quarterly* 27 (September 2016): 599–603.

48. The journalistic account by William Shawcross of the American responsibility for what happened to Cambodia is neither scholarly nor neutral, but it remains a devastating exposure of the unintended consequences of big-power arrogance, ignorance, and lack of sympathy for weak, endangered societies: *Sideshow: Kissinger, Nixon and the Destruction of Cambodia* (New York: Pocket Books / Simon & Schuster, 1979).

49. For some particulars on Pol Pot's education in Paris, see David Chandler's *Brother Number One: A Political Biography of Pol Pot*, rev. ed. (1999; New York: Routledge, 2018), pp. 31–35. In general this book is a good source for understanding the thinking and rise of the Khmer Rouge leadership. On the idealization of communist utopianism in post–World War II French intellectual life, see Tony Judt, *Past Imperfect: French Intellectuals, 1944–1956* (Berkeley: University of California Press, 1992).

50. Ben Kiernan, *The Pol Pot Regime: Race, Power, and Genocide in Cambodia under the Khmer Rouge, 1975–1979* (New Haven, CT: Yale University Press, 1996), and his very comprehensive study of genocides throughout history: *Blood and Soil: A World History of Genocide and Extermination from Sparta to Darfur* (New Haven, CT: Yale University Press, 2007), pp. 540–554.

There is also his earlier *How Pol Pot Came to Power: Colonialism, Nationalism, and Communism in Cambodia 1930–1975* (New Haven, CT: Yale University Press, 1985). See also Kiernan, "The Ethnic Element in the Cambodian Genocide," in *Ethnopolitical Warfare: Causes, Consequences, and Possible Solutions*, ed. Daniel Chirot and Martin E. P. Seligman (Washington, DC: American Psychological Association, 2001), pp. 83–91. During the French colonial period and after, the foremost French academics writing about Cambodia were George Groslier, who was tortured to death by the Japanese in Cambodia in 1945, and his son Bernard-Philippe Groslier. Their intent was to prove to the world and to the Cambodians themselves that their culture and history were of great value and worth preserving. That their ideas were so misused was not their fault. See Bernard-Philippe Groslier, *Angkor: Hommes et pierres* (Paris: Arthaud, 1956).

51. To get at the most likely number, the demographer Patrick Heuveline took all available estimates and older as well as post–Khmer Rouge census data to run sophisticated quantitative reliability tests. He arrived at this number while explaining in great detail that a wider range of half to three times these estimates is possible, but it is only those that cluster around 1.9 million that are most probable. He did the same for the likely number who were directly killed. Heuveline, "Approaches to Measuring Genocide: Excess Mortality during the Khmer Rouge Period," in Chirot and Seligman, *Ethnopolitical Warfare*, pp. 93–108. More recently, Heuveline, "The Boundaries of Genocide: Quantifying the Uncertainty of the Death Toll during the Pol Pot Regime in Cambodia (1975–1979)," *Population Studies* 69, no. 2 (2015): 201–218.

52. The bizarre story of Albania's tribalism, isolation, and autarkic backwardness, and Hoxha's self-deification as well as Albania's outsized role in the complex Sino-Soviet and Soviet-Yugoslav international conflicts, is worth a whole chapter. Barring that, there are some worthwhile sources. Fred C. Abrahams, *Modern Albania* (New York: New York University Press, 2015), pp. 15–27; Blendi Fevziu, *The Iron Fist of Albania*, trans. Majlind Nishku (2011; London: I. B. Taurus, 2016); Donald S. Zagoria, *The Sino-Soviet Conflict 1956–61* (Princeton, NJ: Princeton University Press, 1962), pp. 370–383. A wonderfully written depiction of what it was like in Hoxha's last years is Ismail Kadare's novel about the murder (or suicide?) of Hoxha's closest collaborator and onetime friend Mehmet Shehu, who was then denounced as a spy working for the CIA, the KGB, and Yugoslav intelligence! *The Successor: A Novel* (New York: Arcade, 2005), translated into English by David Bellos from Tedi Papavrami's French translation from the 2003 original Albanian). On North Korea, see the interesting work based largely on Communist Hungary's extensive archives about its relations with other Communist states, Balázs Szalontai, *Kim Il Sung in the Khrushchev Era: Soviet DPRK Relations and the Roots of North Korea's Despotism* (Stanford, CA: Stanford University Press, 2006).

53. Of all the thousands of books on what the Americans call the Vietnam War, three of the best that explain how the United States got into this war are David Kaiser, *American Tragedy: Kennedy, Johnson, and the Origins of the Vietnam War* (Cambridge, MA: Harvard University Press, 2000); Frederik Lodgevall, *Choosing War: The Lost Chance for Peace and the Escalation of War in Vietnam* (Berkeley: University of California Press, 1999); and Lodgevall, *Embers of War: The Fall of an Empire and the Making of America's Vietnam* (New York: Random House, 2012). On the war itself, William S. Turley, *The Second Indochina War: A Concise Political and Military History* (Lanham, MD: Rowman & Littlefield, 2009), and the dramatic Neil Sheehan classic *A Bright Shining Lie: John Paul Vann and America in Vietnam* (New York: Vintage, 1989). On the

French War, see Jacques Dalloz, *La guerre d'Indochine: 1945–1954* (Paris: Seuil, 1987). There is an English translation by Josephine Baker published by Rowman & Littlefield in 1990. An unforgettable Bernard Fall book is essential reading too: *Hell in a Very Small Place: The Siege of Dien Bien Phu* (New York: Harper & Row, 1967).

54. Christopher Goscha, *Vietnam: A New History* (New York: Basic Books, 2016), p. 329 and p. 501n34.

55. Ibid., pp. 290–298 and p. 499nn23–26. Jean-Louis Margolin, "Vietnam and Laos: The Impasse of War Communism," in Courtois et al., *The Black Book of Communism*, pp. 568–570. See also, particularly for some heartbreaking personal stories about this very repressive period, Georges Boudarel, *Cent fleurs écloses dans la nuit du Vietnam* (Paris: Jacques Bertoin, 1991). Boudarel joined the Vietnamese Communists during the French War and participated in abusing and torturing French prisoners of war, the majority of whom died in the prison camps. Later he was a Soviet agent in Eastern Europe before returning to France in 1967, renouncing communism, and having a successful academic career in which he was protected by French far-leftist academics when he was exposed for what he had done. Nevertheless, his book is devastating because of his familiarity with Communist Vietnam, even though he never entirely renounced his past.

56. William J. Duiker, *Ho Chi Minh: A Life* (New York: Hyperion, 2000); Pierre Brocheux, *Ho Chi Minh: A Biography*, trans. Claire Duiker (2003; New York: Cambridge University Press, 2007).

57. The 1964 interview and a general report on North Vietnam by a somewhat clueless French reporter has English subtitles: https://www.youtube.com/watch?v=ROgYHCYU9Zk.

58. Goscha, *Vietnam*, pp. 377–386; Margolin, "Vietnam and Laos," pp. 571–575. On the battle for Hué during the Tet Offensive in 1968, see Mark Atwood Lawrence, *The Vietnam War: A Concise International History* (New York: Oxford University Press, 2010), pp. 122–124. More detail is to be found in Eric Hammel, *Fire in the Streets: The Battle for Hue, Tet 1968* (Pacifica, CA: Pacifica Military History, 1991).

59. Goscha, *Vietnam*, pp. 398–403.

60. Ibid., pp. 123–149 and 190–229, is particularly good in explaining the role of France: failing to take advantage of what could have been a more liberal partnership leading to independence in association with France before World War II, and then launching the "French War" in 1946.

Chapter 5

1. http://www.informarte.mx/gobierno/noticias-locales/el-que-no-transa-no-avanza/.

2. Martin Evans and John Phillips, *Algeria: Anger of the Dispossessed* (New Haven. CT: Yale University Press, 2007), p. 103. On October 5, 1988, large-scale youth riots protesting lack of jobs, economic stagnation, and corruption erupted in Algiers.

3. *Battle of Algiers* is one of the greatest political movies ever made about anticolonial revolutions and urban guerrilla warfare. It is an account of the 1956–1957 FLN campaign of terror in Algiers to persuade the French to leave and the French military's use of torture to break the urban rebels. The French won the battle but ultimately lost the war.

4. Evans and Phillips, *Algeria*, p. 28.

5. Alfred Sauvy, "Trois monde, une planète," *Le Nouvel Observateur*, no. 118 (August 15, 1952): 14. It is the last line: "Car enfin ce Tiers Monde ignoré, exploité, méprisé comme le Tiers Etat, veut, lui aussi, être quelque chose." Robert Malley, *The Call from Algeria: Third Worldism, Revolution, and the Turn to Islam* (Berkeley: University of California Press, 1996), pp. 77–114. For the role played by Sieyès in the French Revolution, see above, notes 13 and 22 to chap. 3 and the accompanying text.

6. Frantz Fanon, *The Wretched of the Earth*, trans. Richard Philcox (1963; New York: Grove Press, 2004). "Preface" from the original edition by Jean-Paul Sartre, and "Foreword" to the 2004 edition by Homi K. Bhabha.

7. Bhabha, "Foreword," p. x.

8. See Evans and Phillips, *Algeria*, pp. 1–66. For more details on the 1954–1962 war, see Martin Evans, *Algeria: France's Undeclared War* (Oxford: Oxford University Press, 2012), and the classic by Alistair Horne, *A Savage War of Peace: Algeria 1954–1962*, rev. ed. (1977; New York: New York Review of Books, 2006). On France's failure after World War II to come to grips with its colonial problems, and how Morocco and Tunisia fared compared to Algeria, see Frank Giles, *The Locust Years: The Story of the Fourth French Republic 1946–1958* (1991; New York: Carroll & Graf, 1994).

9. Evans and Phillips, *Algeria*, pp. 67–101.

10. Luis Martinez, *La Guerre Civile en Algérie, 1990–1998* (Paris: Karthala, 1998). There is an English translation with Columbia University Press, 2000. Evans and Phillips, *Algeria*, pp. 102–214. See also Mohammed Hachemaoui, "La corruption politique en Algérie: l'envers de l'autoritarisme," *Esprit*, no. 375 (6) (June 2011): 111–135. Hachemaoui has a more recent article on how the deep corruption and incapacity of the Algerian regime to govern properly continues. President Abdelaziz Bouteflika, an Algerian War of Independence veteran, remained in nominal power after almost twenty years despite his badly failing health. The ruling military and police were too divided to pick a successor until mass demonstrations in 2019 finally forced their hand. Hachemaoui, "Qui gouverne (réellement) l'Algérie?" *Politique africaine* 142, no. 2 (2016): 169. Adam Nossifer, "Algeria's Ruler, Abdel Aziz Bouteflika, Agrees to Step Down," *New York Times*, April 2, 2019, p. A-9.

11. Ricardo Soares de Oliveira, *Magnificent and Beggar Land: Angola since the Civil War* (New York: Oxford University Press, 2015).

12. On the most recent political changes in Angola, see Norimitsu Onishi, "Angola Holds Ex-Ruler's Son on Fraud Charges," *New York Times*, September 25, 2018, https://www.nytimes.com/2018/09/25/world/africa/angola-corruption-dos-santos.html. Also, "Angola, Party Guy: Why João Lourenço Wants to Be Angola's Deng Xiaoping," *Economist*, December 1–7, 2018, pp. 39–40.

13. Malley, *The Call from Algeria*, pp. 168–203.

14. Mancur Olson, *Power and Prosperity: Outgrowing Communist and Capitalist Dictatorships* (New York: Basic Books, 2000), pp. 111–154. For more thorough analysis, specifically on Africa, see the following notes 15 through 19 and the accompanying text, below.

15. Stephen Smith, in his book *La ruée vers l'Europe: La jeune Afrique en route pour le Vieux Continent* (Paris: Bernard Grasset, 2018), explains some of the dire consequences of Africa's

continuing very high birthrate and poverty and the "scramble" by Africans to get to Europe. Though his book concentrates on sub-Saharan Africa, much of it was applicable for North Africa until fairly recently when birthrates there began to fall rapidly. Algeria's fertility rate in 1960 was 7.52 births per woman. In 2016 it had fallen to 2.78, but there remains a large youth population. Smith's book is controversial but is already being discussed in high policy circles, particularly in France. An English translation was published as *The Scramble for Europe: Young Africa on Its Way to the Old Continent* (Cambridge: Polity Press, 2019). See also Charlemagne (an editorial writer using that name for a regular column on Europe in the *Economist*), "Why Europe Should Focus on Its Growing Interdependence with Africa," *Economist*, September 20, 2018, https://www.economist.com/europe/2018/09/22/why-europe-should-focus-on-its-growing-interdependence-with-africa. For demographic information, see the World Bank data at https://data.worldbank.org/indicator/sp.pop.totl. Then click on specific country names for historical data.

16. There is a huge literature on the subject of what kinds of government and economic policy work best to stimulate economic growth in poorer countries. Is democracy better than autocracy? Can socialism of some sort work, or is it necessary to just let free markets operate? Can some protectionism help, and at what level does it do more harm than good? There is no easy answer about what kind of political system is best, nor what the most optimal balance may be between heavy government intervention and maximal laissez-faire. Some variation seems to depend on specific national cultures, but not entirely. It is clear that one-party autocracies are highly prone to corruption, and when that turns to massive theft of resources, economic development that might benefit the majority of the population is unlikely. See the case studies in *In Search of Prosperity: Analytic Narratives on Economic Growth*, ed. Dani Rodrik (Princeton, NJ: Princeton University Press, 2003).

17. On Africa, see Robert Guest, *The Shackled Continent: Power, Corruption, and African Lives* (Washington, DC: Smithsonian Books, 2004). On the Arab Spring and its aftermath see Mark L. Haas and David W. Lesch, eds., *The Arab Spring: The Hope and Reality of the Uprisings*, 2nd ed. (2013; New York: Routledge, 2018), with special attention to the chapter by Julia Clancy Smith, "Lessons from a Small Place: The Dignity of Revolutions in Tunisia, North Africa, and the World," pp. 10–39. See also Joseph Sassoon, *Anatomy of Authoritarianism in the Arab Republics* (Cambridge: Cambridge University Press, 2016).

18. Jeffrey Herbst argues that what we label corruption in Africa has to be understood as a function of how revenues are generated by a few exported natural resources and in response to political exigencies and expectations. Herbst, *States and Power in Africa: Comparative Lessons in Authority and Control* (Princeton, NJ: Princeton University Press, 2000), pp. 131–133.

19. See the map and individual country scores in Transparency International's 2018 report: https://www.transparency.org/cpi2018. Though Transparency International's measurement method is widely accepted as indicative of real corruption problems, it should be noted that some analysts criticize it. For a critique of the way African corruption is measured, see United Nations Economic Commission for Africa, *Measuring Corruption in Africa: The International Dimension Matters* (Addis Ababa: UNECA, 2016). According to Transparency International, Angola is the 16th most corrupt country in the world out of 180. North Korea is even lower, ranked as tied with Yemen as the 5th most corrupt, and Venezuela is tied for 13th. Algeria is

actually ranked as only 76th most corrupt (tied with Brazil). though its people have been angry with the level of corruption that has been affecting their daily lives for decades. On some of the worst corruption and its effects today, whether in states that claim to still be guided by the revolutionary ideologies of their founders, or others that make no such pretensions such as Afghanistan (9th most corrupt in the world), see Sarah Chayes, *Thieves of State: Why Corruption Threatens Global Security* (New York: W. W. Norton, 2015).

20. On the wastefulness of Ceaușescu's grand public projects, the decay of the Romanian economy, and the chronic shortages in the 1980s, Dragoș Petrescu, *Explaining the Romanian Revolution of 1989: Culture, Structure, and Contingency* (Bucharest: Editura Enciclopedă, 2010), pp. 155–173.

21. János Kornai, *The Socialist System: The Political Economy of Communism* (Princeton, NJ: Princeton University Press, 1992).

22. When I was living in Communist Romania in 1970–1971, I read frequent reports in the newspapers of how petty corruption was being exposed and punished. Those named as guilty were invariably hapless small fry, never anyone important, and the basic system itself was never questioned. The very act of naming a very few unlucky examples gave the impression that aside from these miscreants, that kind of corruption was far from being widespread. But it was.

23. Daniel Chirot, "What Happened in Eastern Europe in 1989?" in *The Crisis of Leninism and the Decline of the Left: The Revolutions of 1989*, ed. Chirot (Seattle: University of Washington Press, 1991), pp. 3–32.

24. The late Karen Dawisha's superbly and meticulously researched book is not the only one to treat this subject, but it is the best so far. Dawisha, *Putin's Kleptocracy: Who Owns Russia?* (New York: Simon & Schuster, 2015).

25. Marci Shore, *The Ukrainian Night: An Intimate History of Revolution* (New Haven, CT: Yale University Press, 2018). Paul Quinn-Judge, "The Revolution That Wasn't," *New York Review of Books* 65, no. 7 (April 19, 2018), https://www.nybooks.com/articles/2018/04/19/ukraine-revolution-that-wasnt/. Perhaps the 2019 Ukrainian presidential election that brought a possible reformer into office will improve the situation, but he faces huge barriers.

Chapter 6

1. *Economist*, October 26, 2017, https://www.economist.com/leaders/2017/10/26/a-tsar-is-born. Cover picture and leading story.

2. Cited in *The Yale Book of Quotations*, ed. Fred R. Shapiro (New Haven, CT: Yale University Press, 2006), p. 441.

3. On the revolutions of 1848 in Germany and much of the rest of Europe, and their failure, Mike Rapport, *1848: The Year of Revolution* (New York: Basic Books, 2009). Also, Jonathan Sperber, *The European Revolutions, 1848–1851*, 2nd ed. (Cambridge: Cambridge University Press, 2005). Major scholarship on the trajectory of German history includes Jonathan Steinberg's *Bismarck: A Life* (Oxford: Oxford University Press, 2011). Bismarck was the ultimate example of the realist conservative who pushed reforms when he saw that repression of liberal and socialist demands would lead only to further instability. Also, David Blackbourn and Geoff Eley, *The Peculiarities of German History: Bourgeois Society and Politics in Nineteenth-Century Germany*

(Oxford: Oxford University Press, 1984). For a belated recognition that perhaps some of Bismarck's legacy was responsible for the disasters leading to Nazism, see the expression of a partial mea culpa (while still anti-Semitic) in a slim book by a foremost nationalist German historian, Friedrich Meinecke, *The German Catastrophe*, trans. Sidney B. Fay (1946; Cambridge, MA: Harvard University Press, 1950).

4. On the use of Bismarck's reforms as a model, see Kenneth B. Pyle, "Advantages of Followership: German Economics and Japanese Bureaucrats, 1890–1925," *Journal of Japanese Studies*. 1, no. 1 (Autumn 1974): 124–164. The quote is from Carol Gluck, *Japan's Modern Myths: Ideology in the Late Meiji Period* (Princeton, NJ: Princeton University Press, 1985), p. 23. For a thorough interpretation of the Restoration, see Alistair D. Swale, *The Meiji Restoration: Monarchism, Mass Communication and Conservative Revolution* (Houndsmills, Basingstoke: Palgrave Macmillan, 2009); Andrew Gordon, *A Modern History of Japan: From Tokugawa Times to the Present* (Oxford: Oxford University Press, 2003), pp. 9–138. The use of the term "Restoration" tries to capture the ambiguous nature of the Japanese *Ishin*, which consists of two Chinese characters that mean "continuity" and "renewal."

5. Chirot, "What Happened in Eastern Europe in 1989."

6. Timothy Garton Ash, *The Magic Lantern: The Revolutions of '89 Witnessed in Warsaw, Budapest, Berlin, and Prague* (New York: Random House, 1990). On Romania, Peter Siani-Davies, *The Romanian Revolution of December 1989* (Ithaca, NY: Cornell University Press, 2005), with pp. 97–101 on casualties. The first Romanian deaths were caused by the security forces firing on protesters, but at the time the number of deaths was wildly exaggerated. Even more deaths occurred after Ceaușescu's fall, though there was no coordinated antirevolutionary repression. See also the references in notes 20–22 to chap. 5, with the accompanying text.

7. On Yugoslavia and the Balkans after 1989, Misha Glenny, *The Balkans: Nationalism, War, and the Great Powers, 1804–1999* (New York: Viking Penguin, 2000), pp. 634–662.

8. Steven Levitsky and Daniel Ziblatt's *How Democracies Die* (New York: Crown, 2018) discusses, among many other cases, the decline of democratic liberalism in Poland and Hungary. The book's main thrust, however, is aimed at explaining what happened to the United States in the late 2010s and the general populist attacks against liberalism everywhere. Specifically on Hungary, Patrick Kingsley, "Hungary's Autocracy beneath a Patina of Democracy," *New York Times*, December 26, 2018, p. A4. On Poland, "Poland's Government Sacks a Third of Its Supreme Court: A Direct Challenge to the Rule of Law, and to the EU," *Economist*, July 5, 2018, https://www.economist.com/europe/2018/07/05/polands-government-sacks-a-third-of-its-supreme-court.

9. Masha Gessen, *The Future Is History: How Totalitarianism Reclaimed Russia* (New York: Riverhead Books, 2017). Anna Politkovskaya, *Putin's Russia: Life in a Failing Democracy*, trans. Arch Tait (2004; New York: Metropolitan Books, 2007). Journalist Anna Politkovskaya was murdered in Moscow, almost certainly on Putin's orders, in 2006. She has not been the only one to suffer such a fate, and each time the Russian government denies involvement. See above, note 24 to chap. 5 and the accompanying text. For a revealing recent story about Russia's state-led corruption, see "The Rise and Fall of Alexander Shestun: A Russian Tale," *Economist*, December 22, 2018, pp. 61–63.

10. On Ukraine, see above note 25 to chap. 5 and the accompanying text. On Central Asia,

see Scott Radnitz's insightful analysis of the misleadingly labeled "color revolutions," in *Weapons of the Wealthy: Predatory Regimes and Elite-Led Protests in Central Asia* (Ithaca, NY: Cornell University Press, 2010).

11. Among the thousands of books about the demise of European communism and its survival in Asia and Cuba, one that nicely summarizes and explains the differences between the various cases is Steven Saxonberg, *Transitions and Non-Transitions from Communism: Regime Survival in China, Cuba, North Korea, and Vietnam* (Cambridge: Cambridge University Press, 2013).

12. Andrei Lankov, *The Real North Korea: Life and Politics in the Failed Stalinist Utopia* (Oxford: Oxford University Press, 2014).

13. See note 8 to chap. 2 above on the Glorious Revolution. David Cannadine, *Victorious Century: The United Kingdom, 1800–1906* (New York: Viking / Penguin, 2017). Why the Industrial Revolution began in England before spreading to most of the rest of Western Europe and the United States has been one of the crucial problems studied by scholars since the mid-nineteenth century. For a good review of the main arguments and a prominent economic historian's new approach, see Robert C. Allen, *The British Industrial Revolution in Global Perspective* (New York: Cambridge University Press, 2009), especially chap. 1, which reviews the major theoretical approaches to this question. An updated, brief history of the Industrial Revolution is Allen's *The Industrial Revolution: A Very Short Introduction* (Oxford: Oxford University Press, 2017). The explanation I like most is in Joel Mokyr, *The Enlightened Economy: An Economic History of Britain 1700–1850* (New Haven, CT: Yale University Press, 2009), and also in his earlier *The Gifts of Athena: Historical Origins of the Knowledge Economy* (Princeton, NJ: Princeton University Press, 2002). On Adam Smith's and other early economists' failure to fully understand the nature of the changes taking place in their own times, see Donald Winch, *Riches and Poverty: An Intellectual History of Political Economy in Britain, 1750–1834* (Cambridge: Cambridge University Press, 1996), pp. 6–8.

Chapter 7

1. Raymond Aron, "Democratic and Totalitarian States," in Raymond Aron, *The Dawn of Universal History: Selected Essays from a Witness to the Twentieth Century*, trans. Barbara Bray, introd. Tony Judt (1996; New York: Basic Books, 2002.), pp. 163–176. The quote is on p. 164. Aron, a sociologist and very prominent public intellectual, lived from 1905 to 1983. As a committed believer in democracy, he fiercely criticized fascism and communism. The quote is from a paper he presented on June 15, 1939. See Stanley Hoffmann's obituary for Aron in the *New York Review of Books*, December 8, 1983, https://www.nybooks.com/articles/1983/12/08/raymond-aron-19051983/.

2. President John F. Kennedy's address on the first anniversary of the foreign aid program for Latin America, Alliance for Progress, on March 13, 1962, p. 21 of the speech's text.https://www.jfklibrary.org/asset-viewer/archives/JFKPOF/037/JFKPOF-037-026.

3. Hett, *The Death of Democracy*, pp. 197.

4. Mancur Olson, *The Rise and Decline of Nations: Economic Growth, Stagflation, and Social Rigidities* (New Haven, CT: Yale University Press, 1982).

5. Along with the already-cited Levitsky and Ziblatt's *How Democracies Die*, a highly recommended analysis that includes Russia's attacks against Western liberalism is Timothy Snyder, *The Road to Unfreedom: Russia, Europe, America* (New York: Tim Duggan / Crown, 2018). Also Barry Eichengreen, *The Populist Temptation: Economic Grievance and Political Reaction in the Modern Era* (New York: Oxford University Press, 2018); and Yascha Mounk, *The People vs. Democracy: Why Our Freedom Is in Danger and How to Save It* (Cambridge, MA: Harvard University Press, 2018).

6. Walter L. Adamson, *Hegemony and Revolution: Antonio Gramsci's Political and Cultural Theory* (Berkeley: University of California Press, 1980).

7. That is a principal theme of Montgomery and Chirot, *The Shape of the New*, particularly in chaps. 5, 6, and 7 on the "Counter-Enlightenment."

INDEX OF CITED AUTHORS

Abrahamian, Ervand, 139n30
Abrahams, Fred C., 150n52
Adamson, Walter L., 157n6
Allen, Robert C., 156n13
Armengaud, André, 136n3
Aron, Raymond, 127–28, 156n1
Ascher, Abraham, 137n17
Ascherson, Neal, 144n31
Asheri, Maia, 139n34
Asselain, Jean-Charles, 136nn3 and 4
Aulard, François-Alphonse, 140n9
Auricchio, Laura, 135n4
Avrich, Paul, 141n16
Axworthy, Michael, 144nn36, 38, and 39

Babel, Isaac, 141n17
Babel, Nathalie, 141n17
Baker, Keith M., 135n3, 137n13, 141n13
Bakhash, Shaul, 139n31
Bartošek, Karel, 136n2
Behrooz, Maziar, 138n29
Bell, David A., 143n26
Berkhoff, Karel C., 146n21
Berlin, Isaiah, 1, 135n1
Bhabha, Homi K., 107–8, 152nn6 and 7
Biard, Michel, 140n4, 141n13
Blackbourn, David, 154–55n2
Bosworth, R.J.B., 139n34
Boudarel, Georges, 151n55
Boudon, Jacques-Olivier, 142nn22 and 26
Bracher, Karl Dietrich, 135n6, 144n34,
    146n18
Brandenberger, David, 148n40

Brinton, Crane, 140–41n11
Brocheux, Pierre, 151n56
Brown, Kerry, 144n35
Brunk, Samuel, 145n5
Buchenau, Jürgen, 145nn6, 8, and 10

Cannadine, David, 156n13
Carlyle, Thomas, 139n1
Chandler, David, 149n49
Charlemagne, 153n15
Chayes, Sarah, 154n19
Chirot, Daniel, 144n3, 146nn19 and 24,
    150nn50 and 51, 154n23, 155n5, 157n7
Chung, Y. David, 147n32
Cipolla, Carlo M., 136n3
Clancy-Smith, Julia, 153n17
Clark, Christopher, 137n18
Clarke, Stephen, 143n28
Cohen, Stephen F., 140n10, 143n30
Conquest, Robert, 146–47n27
Constant, Benjamin, 1, 135n2
Courtois, Stéphane, 136n2, 147nn27 and 31
Cummings, Bruce, 148n37

Dalloz, Jacques, 151n53
Daryaee, Touraj, 138n29
Davies, R. W., 146n25, 147n28
Davies, Sarah, 143n29, 146n25, 148n40
Dawisha, Karen, 154n24
Delorme, Philippe, 140n7
Deutscher, Isaac, 143n31
Dibble, Matt, 147n32
Dikötter, Frank, 148–49n44

Dittmer, Lowell, 148n41
Doyle, William, 136n7
Dubois, Laurent, 142n24
Duiker, William J., 101, 151n56
Duprat, Annie, 141n13
Dupuy, Pascal, 141n13

Edmonds, W. D., 140n6
Eichengreen, Barry, 157n5
Eley, Geoff, 154–55n2
Englund, Steven, 142n25, 143n26
Evans, Martin, 151n2, 152nn4, 8, 9, and 10

Fall, Bernard, 151n53
Fanon, Frantz, 107–8, 152n6
Favier, Franck, 143n27
Fevziu, Blendi, 150n52
Figes, Orlando, 138n25, 147n27
Fitzpatrick, Sheila, 137n17, 138n22, 142n21
Folgarait, Leonard, 145n14
Friedländer, Saul, 146n20
Furet, François, 135nn3 and 4, 136nn3, 4, 5,
    and 6, 137nn9, 10, and 11, 140nn5 and 8,
    141nn11 and 13, 142n22, 143n26

Garton Ash, Timothy, 155n6
Gellately, Robert, 146n18
Gellner, Ernest, 135n4
Gessen, Masha, 155n9
Getty, J. Arch, 147n30
Gheissari, Ali, 138n29
Giles, Frank, 152n8
Glenny, Misha, 155n7
Gluck, Carol, 121, 155n4
Gordon, Andrew, 155n4
Goscha, Christopher, 100, 151nn54, 59,
    and 60
Gramsci, Antonio, 129
Groslier, Bernard-Philippe, 150n50
Groslier, George, 150n50
Gueniffey, Patrice, 135n4, 143nn26 and
    28
Guest, Robert, 153n17

Haas, Mark L., 153n17
Hachemaoui, Mohammed, 110, 152n10
Halévy, Ran, 137n9
Hamilton, Nora, 145n11
Hammel, Eric, 151n58
Hanson, Paul R., 136n1
Hardy, Henry, 135n1
Harris, James, 143n29, 146n25, 148n40
Hart, Paul, 145n5
Hazareesingh, Sudhir, 143n26
Herbst, Jeffrey, 153n18
Herf, Jeffrey, 139n33
Hett, Benjamin Carter, 33, 128, 139nn32 and
    33, 144nn33 and 34, 156n3
Heuveline, Patrick, 150n51
Hilberg, Raul, 146n20
Hitler, Adolf, 145n15, 146n22
Hobsbawm, Eric J., 63, 136n5, 141n12, 144n2
Hoffmann, Stanley, 156n1
Horne, Alistair, 152n8
Hugo, Victor, 143n28

Jackson, Julian, 146n22
Jasanoff, Maya, 139n3
Jospin, Lionel, 143n28
Judt, Tony, 149n49, 156n1

Kadare, Ismail, 150n52
Kaiser, David, 150n53
Katz, Friedrich, 145n5
Keddie, Nikki, 138n29, 139n31
Kennedy, John F., 156n2
Kershaw, Ian, 139n33, 146nn20 and 23
Khrushchev, Sergei, 147n33
Kiernan, Ben, 149–50n50
Kingsley, Patrick, 155n8
Kirby, William C., 148n34
Knight, Alan, 144n4, 145nn11 and 13
Knight, Amy, 147n30
Kornai, János, 114, 154n21
Kotkin, Steven, 82, 143n29, 144n32, 146nn25,
    26, and 27, 147nn30, 31, and 32
Kurzman, Charles, 138n29

Lacour-Gayet, Georges, 142n22
Lankov, Andrei, 125, 156n12
Laqueur, Walter, 144n32
Lardy, Nicholas, 148n37, 149n44
Lawday, David, 142n22
Lawrence, Mark Atwood, 151n58
Lefebvre, Georges, 136n7, 137n10, 142n26
Lenin, Vladimir Ilyich, 12, 136n2
Lenoe, Matthew E., 147n30
Lesch, David W., 153n17
Leuwers, Hervé, 140n4, 141n13
Levitsky, Steven, 155n8, 157n5
Lodgevall, Frederik, 150n53
Lüthi, Lorenz M., 148n39

Ma Bo, 149n47
MacFarquhar, Roderick, 94–95, 148n42, 149n47
Malley, Robert, 152nn5 and 13
Mao Zedong, 36, 139n2
Margolin, Jean-Louis, 100, 136n2, 148nn36 and 37, 149n46, 151n55
Martin, Jean-Clément, 137n10, 140n5, 141n11
Martinez, Luis, 152n10
Marx, Karl, 142n23
Mathiez, Albert, 33, 141n12
Matin-Asgari, Afshin, 138n29
Mawdsley, Evan, 141n15
McDaniel, Tim, 137n16, 138n26 and 28
McLellan, David, 142n23
McMeekin, Sean, 138nn18 and 23
McPhee, Peter, 136n4, 137nn9 and 10, 142n22
Medvedev, Roy A., 140n10
Meinecke, Friedrich, 155n3
Meyer, Jean, 69, 145nn7 and 9
Michelet, Jules, 143n28
Mokyr, Joel, 156n13
Montefiore, Simon Sebag, 144n32
Montgomery, Scott L., 146nn19 and 24, 157n7
Mottahedeh, Roy, 138n29
Mounk, Yascha, 157n5

Naimark, Norman, 147n32
Nossifer, Adam, 152n10

Oliveira, Ricardo Soares de, 152n11
Olson, Mancur, 129, 152n14, 156n4
Onishi, Norimitsu, 152n12
Ozouf, Mona, 135nn3 and 4, 137nn9 and 10, 140nn5 and 8

Packowski, Andrzej, 136n2
Panné, Jean-Louis, 136n2
Petitfrère, Claude, 140n5
Petrescu, Dragoș, 154n20
Peukert, Detlev J. K., 146n18
Phillips, John, 151n2, 152nn4, 8, 9, and 10
Pincus, Steve, 136n8
Pipes, Richard, 137n17
Politkovskaya, Anna, 155n9
Popkin, Jeremy, 142n24
Pyle, Kenneth B., 155n4

Quinn-Judge, Paul, 154n25

Rabinowitch, Alexander, 138n24, 142n21
Radnitz, Scott, 156n10
Rapport, Mike, 154n2
Reynaud, Philippe, 135n2
Richard, Yann, 138n29
Richet, Denis, 136nn3, 4, and 6, 141nn11 and 13, 142n22
Rigby, T. H., 138n21, 142n20
Rodrik, Dani, 153n16
Rothschild, Emma, 135nn3 and 5
Rummel, Rudolph J., 148n35

Salisbury, Harrison E., 148n43
Sartre, Jean-Paul, 152n6
Sassoon, Donald, 139n34
Sassoon, Joseph, 153n17
Sauvy, Alfred, 106, 152n5
Saxonberg, Steven, 156n11
Schoenhals, Michael, 149n47
Schwartz, Vera, 148n34

Seligman, Martin E. P., 150nn50 and 51
Service, Robert, 141n14
Sewell, William H., Jr., 142n22
Shanin, Teodor, 142n19
Shapiro, Fred R., 154n1
Shapiro, Judith, 149n44
Shapiro, Leonard, 138nn22 and 27
Shawcross, William, 149n48
Shore, Marci, 154n25
Siani-Davies, Peter, 155n6
Slezkine, Yuri, 141n17
Smele, Jonathan D., 138n20, 141nn15 and 17,
    142n19
Smith, Adam, 2, 126
Smith, Douglas, 137n17
Smith, Stephen, 152–53n15
Snyder, Timothy, 77, 146n20, 147n27,
    157n5
Soboul, Albert, 137n14
Spence, Jonathan, 91, 93, 147–48n34, 148n38,
    149nn44 and 45
Sperber, Jonathan, 154n2
Steinberg, Jonathan, 154n2
Steinberg, Mark D., 138nn20 and 22, 142n20
Sternhell, Zeev, 139n34
Stites, Richard, 142n21
Sun Shuyun, 148n34
Swale, Alistair D., 155n4
Szalontai, Balázs, 150n52
Sznajder, Mario, 139n34

Tackett, Timothy, 137nn11 and 14, 140n5,
    141n11

Taylor, Jay, 148n34
Tilly, Charles, 140n5
Tocqueville, Alexis de, 136n7
Tomasi de Lampedusa, Giuseppe, 118, 119
Tooze, Adam, 146n18
Trotsky, Leon, 144n31, 147n29
Tuchman, Barbara, 148n34
Tucker, Robert, 143n30
Tulard, Jean, 140n6, 142nn22 and 26
Turley, William S., 150n53
Turner, Henry Ashby, 139n33

Ulrich, Volker, 139n33

Villepin, Dominique de, 143n28

Wajda, Andrzej, 141n12
Walder, Andrew, 149n46
Weinberg, Gerhard L., 146n17
Wemheuer, Felix, 148n44
Werth, Nicholas, 136n2, 147nn27 and 31
Westad, Odd Arne, 148n34
White, Lynn T., III, 148n37
Winch, Donald, 156n13
Wolfe, Bertram D., 138n19
Womack, John, 145n5
Woo, Meredith Jung-en, 147n32
Wood, Gordon S., 137n12

Zagoria, Donald S., 150n52
Ziblatt, Daniel, 155n8, 157n5
Ziegler, Herbert F., 146n16
Zweig, Stefan, 140n6

African anticolonial revolutions and Third Worldism, 106–14
Albania, 98, 121, 150n52
Alexandra of Russia, 21, 23
Algerian Revolution, 105–10, 112
American hostage crisis, Iran, 59–60
American Revolution: English revolutions, influence of, 136n8; Enlightenment thinking and, 17–18; France and, 14; French Revolution compared to, 17–18; ideological essence of, 64; slavery issue unsolved by, 7; traps avoided by, 11
Angolan Revolution, 110–11
anticolonial revolutions, African, 106–14
Antonov-Ovseyenko, Vladimir, 45–46
Arab Spring, 113
Argentina, 77
Armenia, 46
Aron, Raymond, 127–28
Assad, Hafez al-, 112
Atatürk, Mustafa Kemal, 91
Aulard, François-Alphonse, 41
Austria-Hungary, 22–23
Azerbaijan, 46

Bakhtiar, Shapour, 4, 29, 31, 130
Bani Sadr, Abdolhassan, 31
Battle of Algiers (film), 151n3
Bazargan, Mehdi, 59–60
Belarus, 77
Ben Bella, Ahmed, 108–9
Bernadotte, Jean-Baptiste, 52, 143n27

Bismarck, Otto von, 119–20, 154n3
Bolsheviks: Bukharin after Lenin's death and, 40; democratic left and, 131; institutions of repressive control, 43–49, 80; irremovability and, 63; political commissars in Red Army, 53; resistance to, 42; rise of, 23–28; Stalin and, 56; Stalin's purge and, 83–84; Thermidorian reaction, avoidance of, 42; Trotsky and, 53, 55, 56; tsarist secret police and, 43; World War I and, 43. See also Russian Revolution
Bonaparte, Lucien, 51
Bonaparte, Napoleon. See Napoleon Bonaparte
Bonapartism, 51, 53
Boudarel, Georges, 151n55
Boumediène, Houari, 109
Bouteflika, Abdelaziz, 152n10
Brest-Litovsk, treaty of, 43
Britain: changes without revolution, 119, 125–26; defeat of Napoleon at Egypt, 50; English revolutions (1642 and 1688), 125, 136n8; France, intervention in, 38; Iran, intervention in, 29, 30; World War I, 24
Brownshirts (SA), Germany, 58, 74–75
Brüning, Heinrich, 33–34
Bubnov, Andrei, 53
Bukharin, Nikolai Ivanovich, 28, 40, 81, 86, 140n10
Bulgaria, 122
Burns, Ken, 99

cahiers de doléances (Notebooks of grievances), France, 15–16
Calles, Plutarco Elías, 66, 68–71, 73
Cambodia, 95–98
Cárdenas, Lázaro, 66, 71–72
Carranza, Venustiano, 66–68
Casa del Obrero Mundial (COM; House of the Workers of the World), 68–69
Castro, Fidel, 85, 91, 110
Catholic Church: in France, 14, 16, 38, 51; War of the Cristeros, Mexico, 69–71, 145n9
Ceauşescu, Nicolae, 91, 114, 155n6
Central Asian republics, 116, 124
certitude, idealistic. *See* utopian ideologies and tyrannical certitude
Cheka (All-Russian Extraordinary Commission to Combat Counterrevolution and Sabotage), 42–44, 48, 80
Chen Boda, 93
Chiang Kai-shek, 87–89
China: Cultural Revolution, 93–95; fascism in, 87; five-year plan, 90; Great Leap Forward and communes, 90–93; Japanese invasion of, 88; Japanese occupation of Manchuria, 87; in Korean War, 89–90; "Long March," 88; Nationalist/KMT overthrow of Qing dynasty, 86–87; Sino-Soviet relations, 86, 88, 90, 101; survival of communist regime, 124
Chinese Communist Party (CCP), 58–59, 86–94, 101
Chinese Revolution: Maoist utopian ideology and policies, 89–95; moderation of, 94–95; Nationalists, Communists, and civil war, 86–89; People's Republic, founding of, 89; purges, 58–59, 96–97
Chirac, Jacques, 106
civil wars: Algeria, 109–10; China, 88–89; France, 38, 140n5; Mexico, 67–68, 72–73; Russia, 44–46, 141n15; United States, 7, 121; Yugoslavia, 122

class struggle, 80, 82, 89–90
collectivization policy, Soviet Union, 81–83
Comintern (Communist International), 86, 99, 101
communes, Chinese, 92–93
Communist Party, Chinese (CCP), 58–59, 86–94, 101
Communist Party, Iran, 29
Communist Party, Soviet Union, 47–49, 56, 80, 85, 114
Communist Party, Vietnamese, 99, 101–2
Condorcet, Marie Jean Antoine Nicolas de Caritat, marquis de, 1–5, 17, 18, 39, 41, 130
Congo, Democratic Republic of the, 113
Consulate, France, 51
corruption: Algeria, 109, 153n19; Angola, 111, 153n19; Arab Spring and, 113; China, Nationalist, 88; communist economic systems and, 114–15; democratic liberal capitalism and, 133; Eastern Europe, 114, 115, 121; Egypt, 106; as excuse for crackdowns, 39, 58–59; Iran, 7–8, 30, 62; Mexico, 72; one-party autocracies and, 153n16; post-Soviet republics, 123, 124; in revolutionary transformation process, 9–10; Romania, 154n22; Russia, Tsarist, 21, 23; Soviet Union, 112, 114, 115; Third Worldism and, 107, 111–12; Transparency International rankings, 116, 153n19; Ukraine, 116
counterrevolutionary movements: about, 36–37; French Reign of Terror and Thermidorian reaction, 38–41
Cristeros, War of (Mexico), 69–71, 145n9
Cuba, 85, 110
Cultural Revolution, China, 93–95
Czechoslovakia, 44–45, 122

Danton (film; Wajda), 141n12
Danton, Georges, 2, 3, 37, 39–41, 140n9, 141nn12 and 13
deaths and mass casualties: Albania, 85; Algeria, 109–10; Cambodia, 85, 96, 98;

China, Communist, 85, 92–94; China, Nationalist, 88–89; Cuba, 85; France, 6, 37, 41; ideology and, 86; Iran, 59; Jewish holocaust and Nazi-occupied Soviet Union, 77; Mexico, 70, 72–73; Nazi Germany, 77–78; North Korea, 85; Romania, 122; Russia/Soviet Union, 47–48, 77, 82–86, 123, 147n31; Taiwan, 89; Vietnam, 85–86, 99, 100; Yugoslavia, 85. *See also* purges

Declaration of the Rights of Man (France), 17

de Gaulle, Charles, 53, 105, 108

democracy, fundamental theory behind, 4–5

democratic liberalism, 127–31

Deng Xiaoping, 94, 103

Denikin, Anton, 44

Díaz, Porfirio, 65, 67

Directoire (Directory), France, 49–51

Dönitz, Karl, 79

dos Santos, José Eduardo, 110–11

Dzerzhinsky, "Iron" Felix, 43

Eastern Europe, 114, 115, 121–23

East Germany, 122

Egypt, 50, 106, 112

Eisenstein, Sergei, 27

England. *See* Britain

English revolutions (1642 and 1688), 125, 136n8

Enlightenment, 15, 17–18

Equatorial Guinea, 113

Estates-General, France, 15–16

Estonia, 45, 123

Fanon, Frantz, 107–8

fascism: in China, 87; "deification" of leaders, 91; nationalistic war and, 57; as revolutionary, 8, 135n7; rise of, after World War I, 76–77; success of, 77. *See also* Hitler, Adolf; Mussolini, Benito; Nazi Germany

Fascist Party, Italy, 34

fédérés, 19

Finland, 44, 45

First Empire, France, 52

FIS (Front Islamic du Salut—Islamic Salvation Front), 108, 109

FLN (National Liberation Front), Algeria, 105–6, 107, 108, 151n3

Fouché, Joseph, 38

France: Algeria and, 105–6, 108; Consulate, 51; First Empire, 52; First Republic, 37–41, 49–51; Free French Forces against German occupation, 108; Hitler's treatment of, 78; National Assembly, 16, 17; revolutions of 1830 and 1848, 65; Second Empire, 51; Third Estate, 16, 106, 141n13; Third Republic, 39–40; Vichy regime, 78; Vietnam, war in, 99, 101, 151n55; wars of 1792, 18; World War I, 22–23, 24

Franz Joseph of Austria-Hungary, 22

French Revolution: American Revolution compared to, 17–18; Bastille Day and the Great Fear, 16; "Ça ira, ça ira" (revolutionary anthem), 12, 137n15; civil war, 38, 140n5; Condorcet and the La Fayette syndrome, 1–5, 130; conservative resistance, liberal failure, and rise of radical revolutionaries, 13–19; the Directoire and rise of Napoleon, 49–53; effects of, 7; First Republic, Reign of Terror, and Thermidorian reaction, 7, 37–41; foreign intervention, 38; four stages of revolution and, 11; France before the revolution, 13–14; Iranian compared to, 21, 30, 32; Jacobins, 1–2, 18, 28, 38–39, 49; "La Marseillaise," 19; liberal democratic ideals and, 128; Marxist and liberal understandings of, 6–7; Russian compared to, 20, 27–28; Vendée War, 38, 70

Frunze, Mikhail, 45

FSB (Federal Security Service), Russia, 116

Gandhi, Mohandas, 106–7

Georgia, 46

Germany: Bismarkian revolution, 119–20; Lenin, support for, 25; 1948 liberal revolution, 119; Reichstag burning, 57; Weimar Republic, 32–34; World War I, 22–23, 24–25, 43. See also Hitler, Adolf; Nazi Germany

Gestapo (Geheime Staatspolizei), 75–76

Ghana, 112

Girondistes, 39

godlike dictators, 91

Goebbels, Joseph, 33

Gorbachev, Mikhail Sergeyevich, 40, 122

Göring, Hermann, 75

Gorostieta, Enrique, 70

Gramsci, Antonio, 133

Great Britain. See Britain

Great Depression, 32, 33–34

Great Fear, France, 16

Great Leap Forward, China, 90–93

Guinea, 112

Gulag prisoners, 84, 147n31

Haiti, 19, 51–52

Hamilton, Alexander, 18

heroic legends, new, 91

Himmler, Heinrich, 58, 75

Hindenburg, Oskar von, 33, 57

Hindenburg, Paul von, 33–34

Hitler, Adolf: last testament, 63; Mein Kampf, 74, 78, 132; moderates' failure to grasp, 132; Reichstag fire, war, and, 57; revolution and, 8; rise of, 33–34; as utopian ideologue, 64; utopian ideology and racial-purity obsession of, 74–78; violent symbolism, 132. See also Nazi Germany

Hitler Youth, 76

Ho Chi Minh, 85–86, 91, 99–103

Hoover, Herbert, 34

Hoxha, Enver, 85, 91, 98, 150n52

Huerta, Victoriano, 67, 70

Hussein, Sadam, 60–61

ideologies, utopian. See utopian ideologies and tyrannical certitude

Ieng Sary, 96

India, 106–7

industrialization. See modernization and industrialization

Iran: American Embassy takeover and hostage crisis, 59–60; constitution of, 60; interventions in Middle East, 61; Iran-Iraq War, 60–61; Russian, British, and American intervention in, 29, 30

Iranian Revolution: domestic uprisings and, 59; moderation after death of Khomeini, 61–62; Revolutionary Guard, 60, 62; royal incompetence and rise of revolutionary theocracy, 29–32; Russian and French compared to, 21, 30; war and foreign danger, use of, 59–61. See also Khomeini, Ayatollah Ruhola

Iraq, 60–61

Italy, 34, 50, 77. See also Mussolini, Benito

Jacobins (France), 1–2, 18, 28, 38–39, 49

Japan: fascism in, 77; invasion of China, 88; Meiji Restoration, 65, 120–21; occupation of Manchuria, 87

Jews and anti-Semitism: in France, 78; in Germany, 57, 63, 74; Hitler on, 63; in Russia, 47, 55; WWII deaths, 77

Jian Qing, 93

Kadet (Constitutional Democratic Party), Russia, 24, 27, 130

Kahlo, Frida, 73

Kamenev, Lev, 53–54, 83–84

Kang Sheng, 92, 93

Kennedy, John F., 127

Kerensky, Alexander, 4, 25–26, 130

KGB, 43, 73, 115–16, 123

Khalkhali, Sadegh, 59

Khamenei, Ali, 60

Khieu Samphan, 96

Khmer Rouge, 95–98

Khomeini, Ayatollah Ruhola: Bakhtiar and, 4; death of, 61; Iran-Iraq War and, 60–61; moderates' failure to grasp, 132; rebellion, American threat, and power consolidation, 59–60; rise of, 29–32; as utopian ideologue, 64; as *velayat-e faqih* (guardian jurist), 60; *Velayat-e Faqih: Hokumat-e Islami* (The jurist's guardianship: Islamic government) lectures, 31

Khrushchev, Nikita Sergeyevich, 85, 90, 101

Kim Il-Sung and family, 85, 91, 98, 125

Kirov, Sergei Mironovich, 83–84

kleptocracy, 115–16

Knights of Columbus, 70

Kolchak, Alexander, 44–45

Koreans, ethnic, 85

Korean War, 89–90

Kornilov, Lavr, 26

Kornilov affair, 26

Kronstadt rebellion (Soviet Union), 46–47

Ku Klux Klan, 70

Kuomintang (KMT), 87–89

La Fayette, Marquis de, 2–5, 17–19, 41, 130, 137n15, 141n13

La Fayette syndrome, 3–5, 130

Latvia, 45, 123

Lebanon, 61

Le Duan, 102–3

Le Duc Tho, 102

Lenin, Vladimir Ilyich: Baltic countries and, 45; Bukharin and, 40; Cheka and, 42–44; China and, 86; death of, 42, 49; doctrine of revolutionary defeatism, 25; German assistance and repatriation of, 25; Khomeini compared to, 31; Khrushchev on legacy of, 85; moderates' failure to grasp, 132; NEP and, 47–48; on

revolution, 12; rich peasant class, fantasy of, 82; rise of Bolsheviks, 23–28; in Switzerland, 22; Trotsky and, 53, 55. *See also* Russian Revolution

liberal democracy, 127–31

liberalism, classical, 4–5, 7

Libya, 112–13

Lin Biao, 93, 94

Lithuania, 45, 123

Liu Shaoqi, 93, 94

"Long March," China, 88

Louis XIV of France, 14, 15

Louis XV of France, 14

Louis XVI of France, 2–3, 14, 17–18, 20, 38

Louis XVII of France, 38, 140n7

Louis XVIII of France, 140n7

Louverture, Toussaint, 51–52

Machno, Nestor, 46

Madero, Francisco, 4, 65–66, 72, 130

mafia, Russian, 115–16

Manchuria, 87

Mao Zedong: cult of personality, 91; Cultural Revolution, 93–95; death of, 94; five-year plan and Hundred Flowers campaign, 90; Great Leap Forward and communes, 90–93; Lenin compared to, 85; "Long March" and consolidation of power, 88; purges, 58–59, 93–94; symbolic propaganda, 133; as utopian ideologue, 64

Marat, Jean-Paul, 18, 132–33

Marie-Antoinette, 2, 17, 38

Marx, Karl, 51, 53, 80

Marxist-Leninist theory, 46, 54, 80, 93

Marxist theory and history: Algeria and, 110; Chen Boda and, 93; China and, 86, 90, 92; on Girondistes, 39; Gramsci and, 133; NEP, class warfare, and, 79–80; on revolution, 6–7; Shariati and, 30

Mathiez, Albert, 41

Meiji Restoration, Japan, 65, 120–21

Meissner, Otto, 33

Mensheviks, 24, 27, 28, 46, 138n26

Mexican Revolution: chaos, leadership changes, and shifting ideology in, 65–73; United States and, 67–68, 70; War of the Cristeros, 69–71, 145n9

Mexican school of painters, 73

Mexico: civil war, 67–68, 72–73; modernization and capitalist economy, 66; PNR/PRM/PRI, 71; Veracruz, US occupation of, 67–68

Michael of Russia, Grand Duke, 24

Mirabeau, Honoré Gabriel Riqueti, comte de, 41

modernization and industrialization: in Algeria, 109; in France, 2, 20–21; in Iran, 29; in Mexico, 66; without revolution, 126; in Russia, 20–21, 22

monarchy, incompetence of: French, 14–17; Iranian shah, 29–31; Russian, 19–23

Morocco, 108

Morrow, Dwight, 70

MPLA (People's Movement for the Liberation of Angola), 110–11

Mugabe, Robert, 112

Mussolini, Benito: ideology and, 76–77; less violent than Germany, 75; revolution and, 8; rise of, 34; violent symbolism, 132; on war, 57

Napoleon Bonaparte (Napoleon I): against British in Toulon (1793), 38; calendar changed by, 39; impact of, 6–7; Mexican leaders compared to, 71; rise and fall of, 50–53

Napoleon III (Louis Napoleon), 51

Napoleonic Code, 52

Nasser, Gamal Abdel, 106, 112

National Assembly, France, 16, 17

National Convention, France, 37–38, 40–41

National Front, Iran, 29, 31

nationalism: in Eastern Europe, 122; ethnic minorities in Russia and, 20; fascism and nationalistic war, 57; French, 45, 51; German, 26, 79, 120; Iranian, 29, 45; Mexican, 66; rise of fascism and, 76–77; Russian, 45, 124; Vietnamese, 100, 101, 103

Nationalist Party (KMT), China, 87–89

Nazi Germany: human costs of, 77–78; incompetency of conservatives and Hitler's rise, 32–35; as revolutionary, 8; SA and Night of the Long Knives, 58, 75; utopian ideology of Nazism, 74–79; war, foreign threat, and purges, 57–58

Nehru, Jawaharlal, 106–7

Nelson, Horatio, 50

New Economic Policy (NEP), Soviet Union, 47–49, 54, 79–81

Nicholas II of Russia, 20–24

Nigeria, 113

Night of the Long Knives, 58, 75

Nkrumah, Kwame, 112

Norodom Sihanouk, 95

North Korea, 85, 91, 98, 124–25

Novick, Lynn, 99

Nuon Chea, 96

Obregón, Álvaro, 66–69, 71

Okhrana (tsarist secret police), 21–22, 43

oligarchs, Russian, 115–16

Oliveira, Ricardo Soares de, 110

Olson, Mancur, 129

Orozco, José, 73

Orozco, Pascual, 67

Pahlavi, Mohammed Reza, shah of Iran, 29–31, 139n29

Papen, Franz von, 33–34

paranoia, 85–86, 98

Peng Duhai, 93

People's Liberation Army, China, 88, 93

People's Republic of China (PRC), founding of, 89. See also China; Chinese Revolution

Petliura, Symon, 46
Petrograd Soviet of workers, 24, 26, 27
Pius XI, Pope, 70
Poland, 45, 77, 122
Politkovskaya, Anna, 155n9
Pol Pot, 64, 85, 96, 97
Pontecorvo, Gillo, 105
Portugal, 111
purges: China, 58–59, 93–94; Nazi Germany, 58, 75; Soviet Union, 83–85, 147nn30 and 31
Putin, Vladimir Vladimirovich, 116, 123

Qaddafi, Muammar, 112–13

racism and ethnocentrism: American, 7, 67; Cambodian, 96–97; Fanon's condemnation of, 107; Napoleon and, 51; Nazi, 32, 33, 65, 74–75, 78. See also Jews and anti-Semitism
Rasputin, 21–23, 137n17
Red Army, Soviet, 44–45, 48, 80
Red Guard, Russia, 26
Red Guards, China, 93–94
Reign of Terror (France), 7, 38–41
revolutionary defeatism, doctrine of (Lenin), 25
Revolutionary Guard (Sepah or Pasdaran), Iran, 60, 62
revolutions: defined, 5–6; fascism and, 8; four stages of, 8–11. See also specific revolutions by country
The Rise and Decline of Nations (Olson), 129
Rivera, Diego, 73
Robespierre, Maximilien, 18–19, 28, 38–41, 140n9, 141nn12 and 13
Romania, 91, 114, 122, 154n22, 155n6
Roosevelt, Franklin Delano, 71
Rousseau, Jean-Jacques, 19, 96
Russia: abdication of Nicholas II, 24; Iran, intervention in, 30; Kornilov affair, 26; Napoleon's invasion of, 52; 1905 uprising,

21; Okhrana (tsarist secret police), 21–22, 43; post-Soviet, 114–17, 123–24; Provisional Government and political parties, 24–27; World War I, 20, 22–23. See also Soviet Union
Russian Orthodox Church, 137n17
Russian Revolution: civil wars, foreign interventions, and creation of terrorizing state, 42–49; class struggle and, 80, 82; ethnic minorities and, 20, 44, 85, 141n15; French compared to, 20, 27–28; ideology of mature Stalinism, 79–86; Iranian compared to, 21, 30, 32; monarchy and social/political situation leading up to, 19–22; rise of Bolsheviks, 22–28; Stalin's rise vs. Trotsky as potential Napoleon, 53–56. See also Stalin, Iosif (Joseph) Vissarionovich

SA (Sturmabteilung; "Storm Detachment"), 58, 74–75
Saint-Just, Louis Antoine de, 28, 40
sans-culottes (common people), 18–19
SAVAK (Iranian secret police), 29
Savimbi, Jonas, 110–11
Schleicher, Kurt von, 34
Second Empire, France, 51
secret police: Germany, 58, 75–76; Iran, 29; of Napoleon, 38; Russia, post-Soviet, 116; Russia, tsarist, 21–22, 43; Soviet Union, 42–44, 48, 55, 56, 80
shah of Iran (Mohammed Reza Pahlavi), 29–31, 139n29
Shariati, Ali, 30
Sieyès, Abbé Emmanuel Joseph, 41, 50–51, 106, 141n13, 142n22
slavery, 51–52
Smith, Adam, 2, 126
Sokolnikov, Grigory, 53
South Africa, 110–11
Soviet Union: central planning, bureaucracy, and corruption, 112; collectivization policy and famine, 81–83; Commu-

Soviet Union (*cont.*)
  nist Party, 47–49, 56, 80, 85, 114; deaths
  during German occupation, 77; disintegration of, 123; economy, 46–47, 48; industrialization and land reforms, 80–81;
  Jews in, 47; New Economic Policy of
  (NEP), 47–49, 54, 79–81; Sino-Soviet relations, 86, 88, 90, 101; War Communism
  period (1917–1921), 42–49. *See also* Lenin,
  Vladimir Ilyich; Russian Revolution;
  Stalin, Iosif (Joseph) Vissarionovich
SRs (Socialist Revolutionaries), Russia, 24,
  26–28, 138n26
SS (Schutzstaffel; "Protection Squadron"),
  75
Stalin, Iosif (Joseph) Vissarionovich:
  Bukharin and, 40; China and, 88; collectivization policy, 81–83; consolidation of
  power, 49; cult of personality, 85, 91; as
  "godlike," 91; Khrushchev on, 85, 101; military leaders, elimination of, 55–56;
  Okhrana and, 43; paranoia of, 85; peasantry and, 46, 81–82; as political co-
  commander, 53; Pol Pot and, 96; purges
  by, 83–85, 147nn30 and 31; rise of, 53–56,
  143n29; terrorizing institutions and, 42;
  as utopian ideologue, 63, 64
Stolypin, Pyotr, 21–22, 137n17
Sun Yat-sen, 86–87
Syria, 61, 112

Taiwan, 89
Talleyrand-Périgord, Charles Maurice de,
  50–51, 142n22
Thermidorian reactions: China, 94–95; cor-
  ruption and, 10; France, 7, 40–41; Iran,
  61–62; Russian avoidance of, 42; Viet-
  nam, 103
Third Estate, France, 16, 106, 141n13
Third Republic, France, 39–40
"Third World" as term, 106
Third Worldism, 106–14

Tito, Josip Broz, 85, 91, 106
Tocqueville, Alexis de, 15
Tokugawa Shogunate, 120
Touré, Sékou, 112
Transparency International, 116, 153n19
Trotsky, Lev (Leon) Davidovich: exile and
  murder of, 55; Kronstadt rebellion and,
  46–47; Lenin and, 53, 55; Lenin com-
  pared to, 86; as potential Russian Napo-
  leon, 53–56; Red Army and, 44; revolu-
  tion and, 27–28
Tukhachevsky, Mikhail, 45, 46–47, 55–56
Tunisia, 108, 113

Ukraine, 45–46, 77, 78, 82, 116, 124, 154n25
UNITA (National Union for the Total Independence of Angola), 110
United Kingdom. *See* Britain
United States: Angola and, 110–11; Civil
  War, 7, 121; Great Depression in, 34; Iran,
  intervention in, 29, 30; in Korean War,
  89–90; Mexico and, 67–68, 70; Vietnamese refugees in, 103
utopian ideologies and tyrannical certitude:
  about, 63–65; African Third Worldism
  and, 107; Ho Chi Minh in Vietnam and,
  98–104; Khmer Rouge in Cambodia and,
  95–98; Maoism and, 86–95; Mexican
  Revolution as exception, 65–73; Nazism
  and, 74–79; Stalinism and, 79–86

Vendée War, France, 38, 70
Venezuela, 113
Versailles, France, 16
Vietnam: French War, 99, 101, 151n55; Ho
  Chi Minh and revolutionary radicalism,
  98–104; survival of communist regime,
  124; war with Cambodia, 97–98
Vietnam War ("Resistance War against
  America"), 95, 99, 101
Villa, Pancho, 66–68, 72, 145n5
violence provoked by resistance, 6

violent symbolism, 132–33
Volksgemeinschaft, 76
Vo Nguyen Giap, 100

Wajda, Andrzej, 141n12
Washington, George, 18, 72
Whites (Russia), 44–45, 48
Wilhelm II, Kaiser, 23
Wilson, Woodrow, 67
Witte, Sergei, 21
women's rights, Napoleonic Code and, 52
World War I, 20, 22–26, 43–44
World War II, 77–79, 108

Wrangel, Pyotr, 46
The Wretched of the Earth (Fanon), 107–8

xenophobia, 98

Yuan Shikai, 86
Yudenich, Nikolai, 44
Yugoslavia, 77, 85, 106, 122

Zapata, Emiliano, 67–68, 72, 145n5
Zhou Enlai, 94
Zimbabwe, 112
Zinoviev, Grigory, 53–54, 83–84, 86

A NOTE ON THE TYPE

This book has been composed in Arno, an Old-style serif typeface in the classic Venetian tradition, designed by Robert Slimbach at Adobe.